T0202442

Communications
in Computer and Information Science　　1731

More information about this series at https://link.springer.com/bookseries/7899

Valentin Malykh · Andrey Filchenkov (Eds.)

Artificial Intelligence and Natural Language

11th Conference, AINL 2022
Saint Petersburg, Russia, April 14–15, 2022
Revised Selected Papers

Editors
Valentin Malykh
Huawei Noah's Ark Lab
Saint Petersburg, Russia

Andrey Filchenkov
ITMO University
Saint Petersburg, Russia

ISSN 1865-0929   ISSN 1865-0937 (electronic)
Communications in Computer and Information Science
ISBN 978-3-031-23371-5   ISBN 978-3-031-23372-2 (eBook)
https://doi.org/10.1007/978-3-031-23372-2

This Springer imprint is published by the registered company Springer Nature Switzerland AG
The registered company address is: Gewerbestrasse 11, 6330 Cham, Switzerland

Preface

The 10th Conference on Artificial Intelligence and Natural Language Conference (AINL 2022), held during April 14–15, 2022, in Saint Petersburg, Russia, was organized by the NLP Seminar (Russia) and ITMO University (Russia). It aimed to bring together experts in the areas of text mining, speech technologies, dialogue systems, information retrieval, machine learning, artificial intelligence, and robotics to create a platform for sharing experiences, extending contacts, and searching for possible collaboration. Since 2012, the AINL conference series has established a strong foothold in the Baltic region and Russia with a strong focus on research and building resources for local languages. This year our conference also hosted the Russian-English Biomedical Machine Translation Challenge, aiming to improve industry and academia collaboration.

We received 20 research papers. The reviewing process was challenging. We were able to accept only eight long papers resulting in a 40% acceptance rate. We accepted also one long paper from the organizers of the Russian-English Biomedical Machine Translation Challenge and one short paper from its winner. In total, 27 researchers from different domains and areas were engaged in the double-blind review process. Each paper received at least three reviews and almost half of the papers received four reviews. The papers describing the shared task and the winning system are included in this volume after a single blind review by the volume editors. The selected papers were presented at the conference, covering a wide range of topics including sentiment analysis, lexical resources, document retrieval, aspect extraction, dialog modeling, text summarization, text generation, and explainable artificial intelligence. Most of the presented papers were devoted to processing textual data. In addition, the conference program included industry talks from leading companies in the area of text processing.

We are grateful to everybody who submitted papers, who made wonderful talks, and who participated without publication. We are indebted to our Program Committee members for their insightful reviews. We also wish to express our deepest gratitude to our organization team, Anna and Alexander Bugrovsky, for their invaluable efforts during the conference.

October 2022

Valentin Malykh
Andrey Filchenkov

Organization

General Chair

Valentin Malykh   Huawei Noah's Ark Lab, Russia

Local Chair

Andrey Filchenkov   ITMO University, Russia

Program Committee

Elior Vila   University of Elbasan "Aleksandër Xhuvani",
                               Albania
Boris Dobrov   Moscow State University, Russia
Vladimir Ivanov   Innopolis University, Russia
Vladimir Pleshko   RCO Ltd., Russia
Elizaveta Kuzmenko   University of Trento, Italy
George Mikros   National and Kapodistrian University of Athens,
                               Greece
Natalia Loukachevitch   Moscow State University, Russia
Evgeny Kotelnikov   Vyatka State University, Russia
Dmitry Chalyy   Yaroslavl State University, Russia
Anastasia Shimorina   University of Lorraine/Loria, France
Vera Evdokimova   St. Petersburg State University, Russia
Mikhail Alexandrov   Autonomous University of Barcelona, Spain
Denis Kirjanov   Higher School of Economics, Russia
Erind Bedalli   University of Elbasan "Aleksandër Xhuvani",
                               Albania
Dmitry Ustalov   Yandex, Russia
Tatiana Shavrina   Higher School of Economics, Russia
Irina Temnikova   Qatar Computing Research Institute, Qatar
Alexey Malafeev   Higher School of Economics, Russia
Elena Bolshakova   Moscow State University, Russia
Maxim Buzdalov   ITMO University, Russia
Amir Bakarov   Higher School of Economics, Russia
Maria Tikhonova   Higher School of Economics, Russia
Siddhartha Bhattacharyya   RCC Institute of Information Technology, India
Ilseyar Alimova   Kazan Federal University, Russia

Dmitry Kravchenko	Ben-Gurion University of the Negev, Israel
Nikolai Zolotykh	University of Nizhni Novgorod, Russia
Artur Azarov	St. Petersburg Institute for Informatics and Automation, Russia

Contents

Inferring Image Background from Text Description

Dmitry Chizhikov$^{(\boxtimes)}$, Valeria Efimova, Viacheslav Shalamov, and Andrey Filchenkov

ITMO University, 49 Kronverksky Pr., St. Petersburg 197101, Russia
dimkanut@gmail.com, {vefimova,shalamov,afilchenkov}@itmo.ru

Abstract. Over the past five years, text-to-image synthesis has achieved impressive results. However, the generated images are still produced in low resolution and suffer from indeterminacy. In order to improve this situation, we split the image synthesis task into separate parts with predicting the layout of the scene as one of these tasks. We believe that it could be started with the background, which is usually determined by the location of the scene. Given a text, we can try to infer the location described or implied by it. In this paper, we propose two methods for obtaining this information from a given text. The first method called LET (Location Extraction Transformer) is intended to extract the words from a text, in which the scene location is directly mentioned. The second method we propose we call LIT (Location Inference Transformer). It is intended to infer the scene location which is implied by the text, but not mentioned directly. We have also collected two datasets to train and test the corresponding models. These datasets are publicly available at kaggle.com. We have compared the performance of our algorithm with several existing approaches which might be used for extracting the location information from the text. The results obtained by both LET and LIT have occurred to be more superior to other algorithms.

Keywords: Text-to-image generation · Natural language processing · Transformers · Transfer learning

1 Introduction

Automatic generation of realistic-looking high-quality images from the text descriptions (also known as text-to-image synthesis) is a complicated task with a great potential for various computer vision applications, such as photo editing and design creation. Most of the state-of-the-art text-to-image synthesis methods are based on Generative Adversarial Networks (GANs) [15] and Variational Autoencoders (VAE) [9]. Despite recent impressive results [14], producing a complex scene with multiple objects based on the text description remains challenging [42]. GANs for text-to-image synthesis still suffer from a poor image quality [17]. Even state-of-the-art models cannot generate the fine-grained image background [22, 23].

V. Malykh and A. Filchenkov (Eds.): AINL 2022, CCIS 1731, pp. 1–13, 2022.
https://doi.org/10.1007/978-3-031-23372-2_1

To address this challenge, we propose to split the complex task of text-to-image synthesis into some parts [10]: (1) a high-quality foreground image generation and (2) a search of a suitable background image in a database or to generate it with recent state-of-the-art approaches based on Transformer architecture [11].

We define *location* as indoor or outdoor background, which can be a building interior, a geographic point of interest or even general landscape features. In this work, we propose a method to infer the location of the action based on a text description.

Recent scientific studies on natural language processing (NLP) report the outstanding effectiveness of the pre-trained text encoders such as BERT [8]. Moreover, transfer learning based on the Transformer models pre-trained on large-scale corpora demonstrates good performance [24]. Thus, we apply these techniques to our task of location inference.

The contributions of this paper are following:

- We have collected two publicly available labelled datasets. The first one contains natural text with location descriptions[1] and the second one is synthetic[2], based on image captions from Panoptic COCO dataset [26].
- We have suggested a location extraction method based on BERT Transformer model, **L**ocation **E**xtraction **T**ransformer, **LET**.
- We have suggested a location inference method based on BERT Transformer model and Siamese networks, **L**ocation **I**nference **T**ransformer, **LIT**.
- We have compared the suggested models with NER, keyword extraction methods with different embeddings, and generative models.

The structure of the paper is as follows. In Sect. 2, we briefly describe modern natural language processing approaches. In Sect. 3, we present two methods for solving the location inference task. Datasets are described in Sect. 4. Experimental evaluation of both methods is presented in Sect. 5. Section 6 concludes the paper and outlines future research.

2   Related Work

Named Entity Recognition (NER) is an important task of NLP, making possible the detection and classification of entities such as a person, an organization, and a location in any given text. These days, there is a large number of NER software [41]. For example, SpaCy [18] is an open-source library of advanced NLP software written in the Python and Cython programming languages that also offers solutions for NER.

Using NER methods, we can extract only the named locations from the text (e.g. "Northern Sea", "Paris"). However, we want to extract all types of locations.

Keyword extraction is the task of automatic identification of a set of terms (words or phrases) that provide a compact representation of a document content and are explicitly mentioned in the text. Keywords can be extracted using

---

[1] https://www.kaggle.com/viacheslavshalamov/texts-with-locations.
[2] https://www.kaggle.com/viacheslavshalamov/coco-locations.

statistical (such as TF-IDF), linguistic, graph-based, machine learning, or other approaches [3].

Moreover, numerous tasks have obtained significant contributions in terms of performance through the use of word embedding [28]. EmbedRank [4] is one of the state-of-the-art approaches for the keyword extraction task. EmbedRank represents both the document and candidate phrases as vectors in a high-dimensional space. It computes distances between the document and each candidate phrase and selects more closest ones. EmbedRank uses sentence and document embeddings based on Sent2Vec [30].

Keyphrase extraction is quite similar to location extraction since the same locations can be represented as a set of keyword candidates. Therefore, the keyword assignment may be suitable, because we can define a set of location words and find the best suitable location among them.

Generative models have demonstrated impressive efficiency on the text generation tasks, with the state-of-the-art solution being large generative models pretrained on general-domain corpora GPT (Generative Pre-trained Transformer), GPT-2 [36,37], and GPT-3 [6]. Both GPT and GPT-2 models are deep neural network architectures using the Transformer [44], pre-trained on vast amounts of textual data. Fine-tuning GPT-2 pre-trained model can bring substantial gains on many NLP tasks. These days, GPT-3 model [6] with 175 billion parameters is released, but is accessible only through restricted APIs.

BERT. Being based on the Transformer architecture [44], the BERT model demonstrates state-of-the-art results in building the general-purpose vector embeddings for natural language, which are context-sensitive. Despite the fact that BERT has the ability to generate the text, the text produced by GPT-2, which is also transformer-based, has a much higher quality [45].

ROBERTa [29] is based on BERT and was created because BERT was found to have been significantly under-trained and could match or exceed the performance of every model published after it. Therefore, there is a ROBERTa model that uses the modified key parameters, removing the next-sentence pre-training objective and applying training with much larger mini-batches and learning rates. This model achieves state-of-the-art results on benchmarks like GLUE [46] and SQuAD [38].

DistilBert [40] is also based on the BERT model and is lighter and faster. This model has 40% fewer parameters than the basic version of BERT, while it works 60% faster while preserving more than 95% of BERT's highest performance.

LaBSE [13] is also a BERT-based model trained for sentence embedding for 109 languages. The pre-training process of this model combines masked language modeling with translation language modeling.

Transfer learning approach lay in the reuse of knowledge gained while solving a problem and then applying that knowledge to a problem from a different domain. Language models are initially trained on extremely large corpora and achieve outstanding results. However, an entire new model is required for every

NLP task. Thus, a transfer learning is an effective strategy in NLP tasks, because it helps to achieve much better quality [19,39].

Siamese networks [5] is an architecture for a non-linear metric learning through similarity between pairs of objects. The Siamese architectures are good in NLP tasks such as sentence matching and classifying input strings by proximity to the element of a class [33].

The problem of **Location inference** from a text was studied for years already. Some of these studies were associated with terms similar to locations, like *landmarks*. Landmark is a cognitively significant geographic object that is geometrically categorized as a point. Significance of landmark is measured using statistical and linguistic text mining techniques. The paper [43] is devoted to the landmarks and discusses their extraction from the web documents based on users' perception and their usage by people. Nevertheless, this approach can not be applied to the inference of landmarks and does not mention the fact that not in all cases landmarks can be associated with locations.

Other works related directly to locations have proposed various approaches to this problem. In work [21], hidden semantic analysis and ontologies are used to categorize geographic objects from text. However, this approach only manages the 6 location categories.

It is also worth mentioning various studies, which have employed several kinds of social network's post message features to infer the location of online users [2,7,25,32]. They also use NER and POS tagging [27], machine learning and probabilistic methods [25].

In addition to these studies, the paper [35] can be noted. This paper suggests two-layer neural network to learn feature representations, and incorporate the learned latent features into a semi-supervised factor graph model.

Despite the fact, the approaches described in the papers perform high results, the location in these papers is represented by a geographic object, which is closer to landmarks, rather than locations in the representation described in this work.

3   Method

In this section, we suggest two approaches to determine words that describe location in a sentence. The first approach is straightforward and aims to find locations among words in the given sentence. However, sometimes there are no words in a sentence that are directly referred to the location, but the location of the scene is implied. In order to solve this issue and make our model more robust, we suggest to pick the most suitable locations from the pre-defined dictionary of location. In this work, we will define *location words* as the words in the text determining location or words that describe the implied location.

3.1   Searching Location Words in the Sentence

Recently, transfer learning based on Transformer models have significantly outperformed other approaches on various tasks after using pre-trained language models on large-scale corpora [24].

To determine the location words of the sentence, we built a classifier for each token. Firstly, we extract the embeddings for words in the sentence with BERT model to catch contextual relationships between words, which is achieved due to many self-attention layers inside BERT model [8]. Then we apply logistic regression to each embedding vector to classify whether the original word looks like a location or not.

Thus, for each word in the sentence, we estimate the probability of being a location. We denote our method as **L**ocation **E**xtraction **T**ransformer, **LET**.

3.2   Searching Location Words in the Dictionary

Generally speaking, we need to find location words for a given sentence using a whole dictionary (to account for implied locations). For this purpose, we have collected a dictionary of 7000 words and have built a dataset of triplets for negative sampling method [31], the dataset is described in detail in Subsect. 4.2. Each triplet consists of a sentence, candidate word, and a corresponding label. The corresponding label is a binary number that equals one in case of a positive example, meaning that the candidate word is actually a location word for the sentence, and equals zero otherwise.

We use the BERT model again to extract contextual information. However, this time we need to compare a sentence with candidate words using a single vector for the whole sentence. The simplest way to get such a vector is to take BERT output vector corresponding to CLS (classification) token, a special token described in [8]. It was originally used to train the model to predict if one sentence is a logical continuation of another sentence. Therefore, this vector is usually used to describe a sentence.

Then we pass the sentence vector through a fully connected layer with ReLu activation function and freeze weights in the BERT model to stabilize the training process. Freezing weights and adding an extra layer is a common practice to fine-tune a huge model [16,20]. To get a vector representation for candidate words, we pass them through a trainable embedding layer and calculate the dot product between sentence vector and candidate vector. After that, the sigmoid activation function is applied to estimate the probability for the candidate word in order to be a location in the input sentence.

Thus, for each word in the list of pre-defined location words, we can determine how it relates with the text. We denote the suggested method as **L**ocation **I**nference **T**ransformer, **LIT**.

4   Datasets

For training, a large set of data is required consisting of small texts and location labels. For testing, it is also required to have a dataset containing texts close to the real input data for the problem. However, deep models require a large amount of training data. Considering this issue, we have collected a large synthetic dataset.

4.1   Real Texts

We have collected a dataset containing 300 texts from various travel blogs and books, then each text was labeled with one of 20 classes. Most of these texts were used to describe landscapes or surrounding areas. The dataset was split into two subsets containing 250 texts of 20 classes and 50 texts of 12 classes. The first subset contains texts with a location description; the second one consists of texts that do not contain a location.

In the collected dataset we used the most typical location classes found in the existing research [1], based on the frequency of references in the content of blogs. We took 20 the most popular locations from this research, such as: forest, lake, sea, city, mountain, hill, road, urban, building, room, ocean, house, tropic, rain, valley, yard, field, rock. Examples of the dataset items can be found in Table 1.

Table 1. Example of text data in the real dataset. Each record contains text and location labels

Text	Location
It is a collection of buildings, roads laid like a carpet for a queen that will never come	'City'
Rock arose from the ground as if it reached for the sky, peaks of the Alps sculpted by the raindrops...	Mountain
The island is a 45-min ferry from Maui and is home to beautiful beaches...	'Beach'

The dataset was split (see Table 2) because it is a useful indicator of how an algorithm manages the extraction of the location from the text containing it, and how it manages its inferring if there is no explicit mentioning of the location in the text. When testing, splitting into two subsets allows looking not only at the indicators in individual categories but also at the whole picture.

Table 2. Dataset statistics for the two parts: texts with locations, texts without locations, and for the entire dataset.

Part	Objects	Classes
With locations	250	20
Without locations	50	12
Entire	300	20

4.2   Synthetic Texts

We needed synthetic texts to train out model with, thus our approach was the following: The Panoptic COCO dataset [26] was used to create a synthetic dataset large enough to train the deep models. This dataset was not prepared for the task of determining the location from the text, that is why it was necessary to extract a description of the location based on image captions and image segmentation. Image segmentation contains categories of actions and objects contained in captions, these categories were extracted from segmentation; then, on the basis of these categories in captions of images using part-of-speech tagging and manual labeling, information containing descriptions of locations was obtained. After that, on the images from the Panoptic COCO dataset, Image Captioning [34] was applied to obtain additional descriptions, from which locations were selected in the same way. Totally, the dataset consists of 23898 texts and is called **COCO-info**.

However, the location labels in this dataset contained a lot of unnecessary information, which was obtained from image segmentation and could not be referred to as real location. In order to overcome this issue, we applied the information from the research about the most popular queries in photostocks [1]. We made a list of the most popular locations, which had 150 of them; the texts with locations were filtered using this list. This dataset was called **COCO-locations**. Examples of the dataset instances can be found in Table 3.

Table 3. Example of data in synthetic dataset. Each record contains the ID of the image in the original dataset, image caption and a list of extracted locations.

ID	Caption	Locations
500663	The old fashioned train is going over the bridge	'Bridge'
785	A double decker bus is going down a street	'Street'
541055	Several snow skiers are on top of a mountain	'Top', 'mountain'

To train the model for location inference, the synthetic dataset was transformed into a new one, where 15 records were also added with the wrong location for each caption, in addition to each correct location, thus forming the negative examples. 10 of these wrong locations were a random words from the general set of all words in the dataset, and 5 of them were locations that did not describe this text. Thus, more information about the context has been added to the dataset, with the help of which the model can more precisely infer locations in the text. We called this dataset **COCO-locations-NS**. Statistics of the collected datasets are demonstrated in Table 4.

Table 4. Synthetic dataset statistics for the COCO-info, COCO-locations, and COCO-locations-NS.

Dataset	Objects	Unique locations
COCO-info	23898	3675
COCO-locations	12087	150
COCO-locations-NS	893511	7208

The collected datasets were also split on parts for training and testing. Training part is 90% of the original dataset and testing part is the remaining 10%.

5   Results

All experiments were performed on the server with NVIDIA RTX 3090 GPU and AMD RYZEN 9 3950X processor with 16 cores. On this configuration, the LET model was trained for eight hours, the LIT for twelve hours. Implementation is available on Github[3].

To assess the effectiveness of the proposed models, we compare our methods with some of the existing solutions for solving NLP problems, which are capable to solve location extraction or inference task. One of such solutions is the EmbedRank algorithm, which is used for keyphrase extraction.

EmbedRank uses sent2vec embeddings of a given text and keyphrase candidates to calculate the distance between one text and several candidates. Replacing static word embeddings with contextualized word representations has yielded significant improvements on many NLP tasks [12]. Thus, we have tested embeddings of various versions of the BERT model, which were pre-trained for different tasks in the field of NLP and can improve the results. The suggested approaches with EmbedRank with the base and large version of RoBERTa have been compared. We have also tested different versions of DistilBERT that are simpler and lighter than BERT: the base version, the paraphrase version, and the combination of RoBERTa and DistilBERT. Moreover, we have tried the LaBSE embedding, which is a multilingual version of BERT and pre-trained on a larger dataset. All embeddings were used with standard parameters, as the setting had no noticeable effect.

In addition, the GPT-2[4] model, in combination with and without EmbedRank, has been tested. The smallest model with 12 attention modules was used, which was fine-tuned on a small part of the synthetic dataset.

Part-of-speech tagging can also be a solution to the problem; although the location has no specific pattern of parts of speech, it nevertheless needs to be tested. A similar task can be attributed to the recognition of named entities, since named entities can be found as locations; therefore, it is necessary to test solutions to this problem. The spaCy library was used to test both part-of-speech tagging and recognition of named entities.

All described existing solutions were tested on the collected dataset of real texts and testing part of the **COCO-locations** dataset. Testing was performed as follows: we feed the input text into the model, then verify whether the output of the model contains a special label, and then calculate the precision based on the matching of the locations from the output of the model with the locations from the label. For the suggested LET and LIT models and EmbedRank-based models, only 3 the most relevant locations from the output were taken into account. For other models there was no such restriction (all output locations were

---

[3] https://github.com/B-O-O-P/I-know-where-you-are.
[4] https://huggingface.co/transformers/model_doc/gpt2.html.

used). Since we are interested in whether the algorithm is capable of inferring all suitable locations, we used the precision score to evaluate the quality of the models. The results of the testing are presented in Table 5.

Table 5. Precision of testing on the test datasets in percent. The maximum value in the column is marked with bold.

Method	Location extraction	Location inference	Overall	COCO
spaCy	85%	0%	70%	80%
EmbedRank × sent2vec	51%	25%	46%	34%
EmbedRank × RoBERTa Large	34%	15%	30%	22%
EmbedRank × RoBERTa Base	32%	13%	29%	22%
EmbedRank × DistilBERT Base	38%	28%	36%	32%
EmbedRank × DistilBERT Paraphrase v1	38%	19%	35%	33%
EmbedRank × DistilBERT msmarco	40%	13%	37%	33%
EmbedRank × LaBSE	38%	15%	34%	26%
GPT-2	24%	17%	20%	17%
GPT-2 x EmbedRank	26%	18%	22%	19%
LET (Location Extraction Transformer)	95%	0%	79%	94%
LIT (Location Inference Transformer)	35%	30%	34%	88%
LET + LIT	**96%**	**30%**	**86%**	**96%**

Despite the fact that the precision is sufficient to confirm the effectiveness of the suggested models, the F_1-score was also calculated. The calculated F_1-scores are presented in the Table 6.

As it can be seen from the Table 5, based on the results in the inference column, the existing solutions perform poorly for both tasks of location extraction and inference. Moreover, on the basis of testing on texts containing a location, the existing solutions demonstrate insufficiently high precision in the extraction task. However, the EmbedRank algorithm with sent2vec embedding differs from the background of other solutions, showing high results in both tasks. Despite this, both proposed LET and LIT models reveal the highest results in their categories, and combined LET and LIT have the highest precision overall, which proves their effectiveness. However, it is worth mentioning that the data in the training and testing datasets are very different, that is why the results are lower than they can be. This behavior can be avoided by adding more data to the training set.

Table 6. F_1-score of testing on the test datasets in percent. The maximum value in the column is marked with bold.

Method	Location extraction	Location inference	Overall	COCO
spaCy	85%	2%	74%	83%
EmbedRank × sent2vec	52%	25%	48%	18%
EmbedRank × RoBERTa Large	34%	15%	32%	11%
EmbedRank × RoBERTa Base	32%	13%	3%	11%
EmbedRank × DistilBERT Base	39%	30%	38%	11%
EmbedRank × DistilBERT Paraphrase v1	38%	19%	35%	13%
EmbedRank × DistilBERT msmarco	40%	13%	37%	13%
EmbedRank × LaBSE	38%	15%	35%	14%
GPT-2	22%	13%	20%	14%
GPT-2 × EmbedRank	23%	15%	22%	15%
LET (Location Extraction Transformer)	89%	0%	74%	85%
LIT (Location Inference Transformer)	30%	28%	30%	76%
LET + LIT	**91%**	**28%**	**81%**	**88%**

6   Conclusions

Nowadays, despite the fact that many kinds of Generative Adversarial Networks solve the complex task of text-to-image synthesis, they generate unrealistic low-quality images. This paper considers text-to-image synthesis task as group of several subtasks, including finding the key objects of the text and their descriptions. However, the description does not always indicate where exactly the action described in the text occurs. For example, on the beach/in the forest/in the city.

As a result, we have suggested two models for location extraction (if it is contained in a text) and location inference (if it is not described in a text) based on BERT model. Moreover, we have compared suggested models with the keywords extraction approach and tried to generate the missing parts of the text. The comparison has revealed that the suggested models are better for both tasks.

The proposed methods can be improved by expanding the training dataset, since locations can be unexpected phrases that are not contained in the current dataset, and in this case, the probability of determining the location will be quite low. To better assess quality of the proposed method, we plan to collect natural annotations from large corpora using the list of location words.

References

1. Top 1000 phrases that customers use to buy images (market research) (2020). https://www.microstockgroup.com/general-stock-discussion/top-phrases-that-customers-use-to-buy-images-(market-research)

2. Ajao, O., Hong, J., Liu, W.: A survey of location inference techniques on twitter. J. Inf. Sci. **41**(6), 855–864 (2015)
3. Beliga, S., Meštrović, A., Martinčić-Ipšić, S.: An overview of graph-based keyword extraction methods and approaches. J. Inf. Organ. Sci. **39**(1), 1–20 (2015)
4. Bennani-Smires, K., Musat, C., Hossmann, A., Baeriswyl, M., Jaggi, M.: Simple unsupervised keyphrase extraction using sentence embeddings. arXiv preprint arXiv:1801.04470 (2018)
5. Bromley, J., Guyon, I., LeCun, Y., Säckinger, E., Shah, R.: Signature verification using a "siamese" time delay neural network. In: Advances in Neural Information Processing Systems 6, pp. 737–744 (1993)
6. Brown, T.B., et al.: Language models are few-shot learners. arXiv preprint arXiv:2005.14165 (2020)
7. Chang, H.W., Lee, D., Eltaher, M., Lee, J.: @Phillies tweeting from Philly? Predicting twitter user locations with spatial word usage. In: 2012 IEEE/ACM International Conference on Advances in Social Networks Analysis and Mining, pp. 111–118. IEEE (2012)
8. Devlin, J., Chang, M.W., Lee, K., Toutanova, K.: BERT: pre-training of deep bidirectional transformers for language understanding. arXiv preprint arXiv:1810.04805 (2018)
9. Doersch, C.: Tutorial on variational autoencoders. arXiv preprint arXiv:1606.05908 (2016)
10. Efimova, V., Filchenkov, A.: Text-based sequential image generation. In: Fourteenth International Conference on Machine Vision (ICMV 2021), vol. 12084, pp. 125–132. SPIE (2022)
11. Esser, P., Rombach, R., Ommer, B.: Taming transformers for high-resolution image synthesis. In: Proceedings of the IEEE/CVF Conference on Computer Vision and Pattern Recognition, pp. 12873–12883 (2021)
12. Ethayarajh, K.: How contextual are contextualized word representations? Comparing the geometry of BERT, ELMo, and GPT-2 embeddings. arXiv preprint arXiv:1909.00512 (2019)
13. Feng, F., Yang, Y., Cer, D., Arivazhagan, N., Wang, W.: Language-agnostic BERT sentence embedding. arXiv preprint arXiv:2007.01852 (2020)
14. Frolov, S., Hinz, T., Raue, F., Hees, J., Dengel, A.: Adversarial text-to-image synthesis: a review. arXiv preprint arXiv:2101.09983 (2021)
15. Goodfellow, I.J., et al.: Generative adversarial networks. arXiv preprint arXiv:1406.2661 (2014)
16. Hendrycks, D., Liu, X., Wallace, E., Dziedzic, A., Krishnan, R., Song, D.: Pretrained transformers improve out-of-distribution robustness. arXiv preprint arXiv:2004.06100 (2020)
17. Hinz, T., Heinrich, S., Wermter, S.: Semantic object accuracy for generative text-to-image synthesis. arXiv preprint arXiv:1910.13321 (2019)
18. Honnibal, M., Montani, I.: spaCy 2: natural language understanding with Bloom embeddings, convolutional neural networks and incremental parsing (2017, to appear)
19. Houlsby, N., et al.: Parameter-efficient transfer learning for NLP. In: International Conference on Machine Learning, pp. 2790–2799. PMLR (2019)
20. Howard, J., Ruder, S.: Universal language model fine-tuning for text classification. arXiv preprint arXiv:1801.06146 (2018)
21. Huang, Y.: Conceptually categorizing geographic features from text based on latent semantic analysis and ontologies. Ann. GIS **22**(2), 113–127 (2016)

22. Karras, T., Laine, S., Aila, T.: A style-based generator architecture for generative adversarial networks. In: Proceedings of the IEEE/CVF Conference on Computer Vision and Pattern Recognition, pp. 4401–4410 (2019)

23. Karras, T., Laine, S., Aittala, M., Hellsten, J., Lehtinen, J., Aila, T.: Analyzing and improving the image quality of styleGAN. In: Proceedings of the IEEE/CVF Conference on Computer Vision and Pattern Recognition, pp. 8110–8119 (2020)

24. Lee, J.S., Hsiang, J.: Patent claim generation by fine-tuning OpenAI GPT-2. World Patent Inf. **62**, 101983 (2020) .

25. Li, R., Wang, S., Deng, H., Wang, R., Chang, K.C.C.: Towards social user profiling: unified and discriminative influence model for inferring home locations. In: Proceedings of the 18th ACM SIGKDD International Conference on Knowledge Discovery and Data Mining, pp. 1023–1031 (2012)

26. Lin, T.-Y., et al.: Microsoft COCO: common objects in context. In: Fleet, D., Pajdla, T., Schiele, B., Tuytelaars, T. (eds.) ECCV 2014. LNCS, vol. 8693, pp. 740–755. Springer, Cham (2014). https://doi.org/10.1007/978-3-319-10602-1_48

27. Lingad, J., Karimi, S., Yin, J.: Location extraction from disaster-related microblogs. In: Proceedings of the 22nd International Conference on World Wide Web, pp. 1017–1020 (2013)

28. Liu, X., He, P., Chen, W., Gao, J.: Multi-task deep neural networks for natural language understanding. arXiv preprint arXiv:1901.11504 (2019)

29. Liu, Y., et al.: RoBERTa: a robustly optimized BERT pretraining approach. arXiv preprint arXiv:1907.11692 (2019)

30. Mikolov, T., Chen, K., Corrado, G., Dean, J.: Efficient estimation of word representations in vector space. arXiv preprint arXiv:1301.3781 (2013)

31. Mikolov, T., Sutskever, I., Chen, K., Corrado, G., Dean, J.: Distributed representations of words and phrases and their compositionality. arXiv preprint arXiv:1310.4546 (2013)

32. Miura, Y., Taniguchi, M., Taniguchi, T., Ohkuma, T.: Unifying text, metadata, and user network representations with a neural network for geolocation prediction. In: Proceedings of the 55th Annual Meeting of the Association for Computational Linguistics (Volume 1: Long Papers), pp. 1260–1272 (2017)

33. Neculoiu, P., Versteegh, M., Rotaru, M.: Learning text similarity with siamese recurrent networks. In: Proceedings of the 1st Workshop on Representation Learning for NLP, pp. 148–157 (2016)

34. Oriol, V., Alexander, T., Samy, B., Dumitru, E.: Show and tell: a neural image caption generator. arXiv preprint arXiv:1411.4555v2 (2015)

35. Qian, Y., Tang, J., Yang, Z., Huang, B., Wei, W., Carley, K.M.: A probabilistic framework for location inference from social media. arXiv preprint arXiv:1702.07281 (2017)

36. Radford, A., Narasimhan, K., Salimans, T., Sutskever, I.: Improving language understanding by generative pre-training (2018)

37. Radford, A., Wu, J., Child, R., Luan, D., Amodei, D., Sutskever, I.: Language models are unsupervised multitask learners. OpenAI Blog **1**(8), 9 (2019)

38. Rajpurkar, P., Jia, R., Liang, P.: Know what you don't know: unanswerable questions for squad. arXiv preprint arXiv:1806.03822 (2018)

39. Ruder, S., Peters, M.E., Swayamdipta, S., Wolf, T.: Transfer learning in natural language processing. In: Proceedings of the 2019 Conference of the North American Chapter of the Association for Computational Linguistics: Tutorials, pp. 15–18 (2019)

40. Sanh, V., Debut, L., Chaumond, J., Wolf, T.: DistilBERT, a distilled version of BERT: smaller, faster, cheaper and lighter. arXiv preprint arXiv:1910.01108v4 (2020)
41. Schmitt, X., Kubler, S., Robert, J., Papadakis, M., LeTraon, Y.: A replicable comparison study of NER software: StanfordNLP, NLTK, OpenNLP, SpaCy, Gate. In: 2019 Sixth International Conference on Social Networks Analysis, Management and Security (SNAMS), pp. 338–343. IEEE (2019)
42. Sylvain, T., Zhang, P., Bengio, Y., Hjelm, R.D., Sharma, S.: Object-centric image generation from layouts. arXiv preprint arXiv:2003.07449 (2020)
43. Tezuka, T., Tanaka, K.: Landmark extraction: a web mining approach. In: Cohn, A.G., Mark, D.M. (eds.) COSIT 2005. LNCS, vol. 3693, pp. 379–396. Springer, Heidelberg (2005). https://doi.org/10.1007/11556114_24
44. Vaswani, A., et al.: Attention is all you need. arXiv preprint arXiv:1706.03762 (2017)
45. Wang, A., Cho, K.: BERT has a mouth, and it must speak: BERT as a Markov random field language model. arXiv preprint arXiv:1902.04094 (2019)
46. Wang, A., Singh, A., Michael, J., Hill, F., Levy, O., Bowman, S.R.: GLUE: a multi-task benchmark and analysis platform for natural language understanding. arXiv preprint arXiv:1804.07461 (2018)

Topical Extractive Summarization

Kristina Zheltova[1]([✉])[iD], Anastasia Ianina[2][iD], and Valentin Malykh[3][iD]

[1] ITMO University, Saint Petersburg, Russia
masterkristall@gmail.com
[2] Moscow Institute of Physics and Technology, Moscow, Russia
yanina@phystech.edu
[3] Kazan Federal University, Kazan, Russia
valentin.malykh@phystech.edu

Abstract. In this paper we propose a graph-based biased LexRank approach combined with topic modeling to create a topic-based extractive summarization model. Topical summarization task is used to obtain a customized summary for a particular reader. We achieve so by including information about topics of interest into an extractive summarization model. Topical information is derived via aspect embedding vectors from the ABAE model and used as a topic input for the biased LexRank model that runs on the heterogeneous graph of topics and sentences. Inclusion of the topical structure into a summary increases the targeting of the summary and makes the overall summarization model benefit from it. We conduct experiments on a novel dataset for extractive summarization quality evaluation constructed by ourselves from Wikipedia articles.

Keywords: Topical summarization · Text summarization · Extractive summary · Topic modeling

1 Introduction

Text summarization task is a process of shortening a source text while preserving its main informative value. Getting a short text description is applicable to information retrieval, question answering, reading comprehension and many other tasks in Natural Language Processing. However, manual text summarization is a time-consuming and routine task. Thus, automation of it constitutes a strong motivation for academic research.

Typically, text summarization techniques are divided into abstractive and extractive approaches. The abstractive method deals with generating short summaries with ideas from the source text, but in completely novel words. The extractive approach retrieves the most relevant sentences from a text when each sentence is visited sequentially in the original document order, and a binary decision is made in terms of whether or not it should be included in the summary. Thus, topical extractive summarization is directed towards labeling sentences relevancy to a given topic.

V. Malykh and A. Filchenkov (Eds.): AINL 2022, CCIS 1731, pp. 14–26, 2022.
https://doi.org/10.1007/978-3-031-23372-2_2

However, one text can cover a big set of semantic aspects or topics, which may possess different levels of interest for different readers. We contribute to this direction by proposing a summarization approach that helps to obtain a customized summary for a reader with a particular information demand.

We propose a modernized LexRank approach to extractive text summarization that bridges the gap between topic modeling and automatic text summarization. We enhance biased LexRank algorithm [5] with the topical information about the aspects retrieved from texts with Attention-based Aspect Extraction (ABAE) model [6]. Our experiments show that inclusion of topical information could potentially increase the targeting of the summary making the overall summary quality benefit from it too.

Our second contribution stems from creating a new dataset for extractive summarization. We modify WikiPersons dataset to use it for topical summarization. We do so by matching headlines with the retrieved topics manually.

2   Related Work

It is clear that the same text can be summarized in different ways, depending on the preferences of the user. For example, one piece of news may contain political and economic content. There are many ways of creating an extractive summary from a source text. However, there were very few attempts in extractive summarization techniques considering topical information of the text corpora.

In the work [15] authors present Recurrent Neural Network based on sequence model for extractive summarization. The work focuses only on sentential extractive summarization of single documents using neural networks. GRU [2] was used as the basic building block of the sequence classifier. This model contributes to the direction of aspect-based summaries by taking into account and visualizing abstract features such as information content, salience and novelty.

In the [22] the discourse-aware neural extractive summarization model was built upon BERT. To perform compression with extraction simultaneously and reduce redundancy across sentences, authors take Elementary Discourse Unit (EDU) as the minimal selection unit (instead of a sentence) for extractive summarization. Extractive summarization is formulated as a sequential labeling task, where each EDU is scored by neural networks, and decisions are made based on the scores of all EDUs.

The work [14] describes TextRank - a graph-based ranking model for text processing and sentence extraction. The basic idea is that when one vertex in linked to another one, it is basically casting a vote for that other vertex. The higher the number of votes casting for a vertex, the higher the importance of the vertex.

In the [23] the first step is producing a sentence relation graph. Given a relation graph, their summarization model applies a Graph Convolutional Network (GCN) [10], which takes in sentence embeddings from a Recurrent Neural Network. Then sentence salience estimations are obtained via a regression. It allows to extract relevant sentences in a greedy manner avoiding redundancy.

The authors of [5] propose a graph-based sentence ranking algorithm for extractive summarization. This method is a version of the LexRank algorithm extended to the focused summarization task of DUC 2006. As in LexRank, the set of sentences in a document cluster is represented as a graph, where nodes are sentences and links between the nodes are induced by a similarity relation between the sentences. Then authors perform the ranking of the sentences according to a random walk model defined in terms of both the inter-sentence similarities and the similarities of the sentences to the topic description.

The [3] paper proposes a graph neural network (GNN)-based extractive summarization model, enabling to capture inter-sentence relationships efficiently via graph-structured document representation. This model integrates a joint neural topic model (NTM) to discover latent topics, which can provide document-level features for sentence selection.

One of the recent works [1] proposes text summarization approach that incorporates topic modeling and a specifically designed semantic measure within the vector space model. They generate extractive summaries of a good quality including only those sentences into the summary, which represent the maximum number of the document topics.

As a part of our experimentation we test different topic models including additively regularized ones [20] trained using library called BigARTM [19]. We also test several neural topic models including NVDM [13], GSM [12] and ETM [4]. The results of the experiments are presented in Sect. A.

3   Model Description

Our main proposition is to include topical information in the extractive summarization model. It is possible to use word embeddings for top-tokens from topic modeling (i.e. words with max probability) or for aspects from aspect modeling as a topic description for biased LexRank algorithm [5] on heterogeneous graph. We use Attention-based Aspect Extraction (ABAE) [6] model to produce sentence and aspects embeddings, although any topic model can be used to produce topics vectors.

3.1   ABAE

ABAE [6] is a neural network based approach with the aim of discovering coherent aspects. The model improves coherence by exploiting the distribution of word co-occurrences through the use of neural word embeddings. Unlike topic models which typically assume independently generated words, word embedding models encourage words that appear in similar contexts to be located close to each other in the embedding space. Thus, ABAE learns a set of aspect embeddings, where each aspect can be interpreted by looking at the nearest words located in the same embedding space. It successfully captures word co-occurrences and also overcomes the problem of data sparsity.

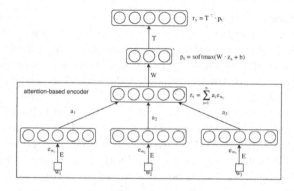

Fig. 1. An example of the ABAE structure [6]

The process of obtaining aspect embeddings in ABAE model starts with neural word embeddings that map co-occurring words into nearby points in the embedding space. After that word embeddings are filtered within a sentence using an attention mechanism and are used to construct aspects vectors. In fact, the training process is analogous to auto-encoders training. After obtaining the sentence embedding it is possible to compute the reconstruction of the sentence embedding which is a linear combination of aspect embeddings. During training ABAE uses two-component loss function, which is aimed at minimizing the reconstruction error:

$$L(\theta) = J(\theta) + \lambda U(\theta) \tag{1}$$

where $J(\theta)$ is a hinge loss that maximizes the inner product between reconstructed sentence embedding r_s and target sentence embedding z_s and simultaneously minimizes the inner product between r_s and the negative samples:

$$J(\theta) = \sum_{s \in D} \sum_{i=1}^{m} max(0, 1 - r_s z_s + r_s n_i) \tag{2}$$

where D represents the training data set and θ represents the model parameters. Other loss part $U(\theta)$ is regularization term, which is used to achieve aspects diversity:

$$U(\theta) = \|\mathbf{T}_n \cdot \mathbf{T}_n^\top - \mathbf{I}\| \tag{3}$$

where I is an identity matrix, T is an aspect embedding matrix and T_n is T with each row normalized to have length 1. The aforementioned contrastive max-margin objective function was used in a several previous works [8,18,21]. After training we can obtain a set of aspect embeddings and sentence embeddings reconstructed from aspect embeddings. An example of ABAE structure is shown in Fig. 1.

3.2   Heterogeneous LexRank

The next stage is based on heterogeneous graph and an algorithm called LexRank [5]. Basic LexRank is a stochastic graph-based method for computing relative importance of textual blocks. In this method the sentence importance is computed based on the concept of eigenvector centrality in a graph representation of sentences. Adjacency matrix is computed as a connectivity matrix based on intra-sentence cosine similarity between sentences. It is important to notice that LexRank is robust to the noise in the data which may be explained by the imperfect topical clustering of the documents. Finally, LexRank values can be computed via an iterative routine called the power method. Power method is an iterative numerical method. Given a diagonalizable matrix A, the algorithm will produce a number λ, which is the greatest (in absolute value) eigenvalue of A, and a nonzero vector v, which is a corresponding eigenvector of λ.

Biased LexRank [16] is a method for semi-supervised passage retrieval that represents a text as a graph of text blocks linked based on their pairwise lexical similarity. The process of finding semantically close text blocks is performed via random walk on the lexical similarity graph. All in all, Biased LexRank is a variation of the LexRank algorithm, where all the nodes are divided into sentence-level and aspect-level ones, links between the nodes are induced by a similarity relation between the sentences on the one hand and between a particular sentence and a topic on the other hand. This algorithm was tested in [16] and showed its top-notch performance not only for topic-focused text summarization task, but also for question answering task.

We modify Biased LexRank in such a way that a Biased LexRank model is fed with the heterogeneous graph. After that, we can perform random walking: the process starts at a random sentence and then at each step with probability d goes to a random node or with probability $(1 - d)$ goes to an adjacent node.

Such an adopted Biased LexRank with heterogeneous graph can be computed as follows:

$$LR(u|t) = d * cos(u, t) + (1 - d) * \sum_{v \in adj[u]} \frac{cos(u, v)}{\sum_{z \in adj[v]} cos(v, z)} * LR(v|t) \quad (4)$$

where t is a vector of the topic, u is a vector of a sentence, cos is cosine similarity.

4 Datasets

4.1 Our New Dataset Constructed from WikiPersons

We propose to modify WikiPersons dataset in order to use its contents for extractive summarization. To form a query-based (or in our case topic-based) summarization dataset automatically from Wikipedia articles, one can take the body text of citation as the document and the article title along with section titles to form a query. Such supporting citations are expected to provide an adequate context to derive the statement, thus can serve as the source document. On the other hand, the section titles give a hint about which aspect of the document the summary should be focusing on, making them an ideal candidate to form a query. For example, the highlighted statement from an example of WikiPersons

```
"2 Chainz": {
  "Детство": {
    "text": [
      "Таухид Эппс родился в Колледж-Парке, Джорджия.[3] Он обучался в Средней школе Севернго
      Клейтона, где играл в баскетбол и занял второе место в своём классе. В старших классах
      он баловался марихуаной и потом, в возрасте 15 лет, его поймали за хранение кокаина.[4]
      Позже он продолжил обучение в Алабамском университете, там молодой Эппс играл в
      баскетбольной команде с 1995 по 1997 год.[5][6] Из 35 игр, в среднем он получал 45,8
      очков, 11 из которых были передачами и 10,6 подборами.[5]\n",
      "На интервью у известного музыкального журнала Rolling Stone его спросили о давних слухах,
      что он окончил Алабамский университет со средней оценкой 4.0 по GPA, о котором много
      говорили во всех информационных порталах, в том числе и Википедии, 2 Chainz сказал: «Не
      верьте Wack-ipedia. Там много ложных вещей, до такой степени, что каждый раз, когда я
      пытаюсь исправить одну вещь, появляется что-то ещё.»[7] Фактически, он перешёл в
      Университет штата Вирджинии из-за обстоятельств, о которых он не охотно говорил. «Я
      попал в беду, пошел куда-то ещё и вернулся, но я окончил школу, и все. Так всё было»,-
      говорил он.[4]\n"
    ],
    "topic_num": 34
  },
  "Семья": {
    "text": [
      "У Эппса две дочери: Heaven и Harmony. 14 октября 2015 года 2 Chainz приветствовал своего
      третьего ребёнка под именем Halo.\n"
    ],
    "topic_num": 2
  }
},
```

Fig. 2. WikiPersons dataset example

dataset (Fig. 2) can be treated as a summary, while the concatenated section titles may act as a query. In this example Wikipedia page about 2 Chainz contains two topics with the assigned texts that can be treated as golden summaries for the topics.

Given that Wikipedia is the largest online encyclopedia, massive query-focused summarization examples can be automatically constructed. For instance, such an approach is adopted in [25], where the authors collected a large query-focused summarization dataset named WikiRef of more than 280,000 examples.

In order to construct our own dataset, we take 10,400 pages from the Personalities category from Russian Wikipedia. We consider each headline as a short topic description. For example, treating one personal page as a whole text, it is possible to highlight such headings as "family and childhood", "beginning of a career", "legacy" and so on, which will be topics descriptions. When the topic modeling process is done, headlines are matched with topics manually. Some headlines with unclear meaning or with low frequency in the corpus were ignored. After such filtering, the resulting dataset contains 7333 short texts with one or more assigned topics. Manual matching of headlines and topics was performed for headlines with a frequency of at least 50. Finally, let us summarize the main dataset statistics:

- Headline length: 3,43 tokens on average.
- Text length: 401 tokens on average.
- Train-set: 5000 texts, test-set: 2333 texts.

5   Experiments

All the experiments from this section are conducted using the novel dataset constructed by ourselves based on the WikiPersons data.

5.1   Evaluation Metrics

Next we provide a quantitative evaluation of the proposed method using the following set of metrics.

First, we calculate the precision of extractive summarization. Precision is a proportion of sentences really belonging to a given topic regarding all sentences that are related to this topic. Precision is calculated for each document independently. Second, we used full-length F1-scores of ROUGE-1 and ROUGE-2 [11] for evaluation:

$$ROUGE_N = \frac{\sum_{S \in R} \sum_{s_n \in S} count_{match}(s_n)}{\sum_{S \in R} \sum_{s_n \in S} count(s_n)} \tag{5}$$

where n is the length of the n-gram s_n, and $count_{match}(s_n)$ is the maximum number of n-grams co-occurring in a candidate summary and a set of reference summaries R.

For the experiments in the Appendix A.2 we also used pointwise mutual information and normalized pointwise mutual information for evaluating the quality of neural topic models:

$$PMI(x, y) = \log_2 \frac{p(x, y)}{p(x)p(y)} = \log_2 \frac{p(x|y)}{p(x)} = \log_2 \frac{p(y|x)}{p(y)}; \tag{6}$$

$$NPMI(x, y) = \frac{PMI(x, y)}{\log_2(p(x, y))}, \tag{7}$$

where $x \sim X$, $y \sim Y$, X and Y—two independent random variable.

5.2   Experiments with ABAE and Heterogeneous LexRank

We compared several experiment setups:

– graph consisting of all sentence nodes and all aspects nodes (#**1**);
– graph consisting of all sentence nodes and a single target aspect node (#**2**);
– graph consisting of all sentence nodes and all aspects nodes with an emphasis on target aspect (just adding coefficient of multiplication) (#**3**);
– graph consisting of all sentence nodes and a single target aspect node with an emphasis on target aspect (#**4**).

In fact, all these experiments only differ in the set of nodes and the presence or absence of the target aspect emphasis.

Table 1. ROUGE-1 for Heterogeneous LexRank on WikiPersons dataset

#	Precision	ROUGE-1 (precision)	ROUGE-1 (recall)	ROUGE-1 (F1)
1	0.69735	0.93009	0.33000	0.41883
2	0.69632	**0.93047**	0.33114	0.42002
3	0.69841	0.93037	0.33133	0.42016
4	**0.69906**	0.92965	**0.33177**	**0.42093**

Table 2. ROUGE-2 for heterogeneous LexRank on WikiPersons dataset

#	ROUGE-2 (precision)	ROUGE-2 (recall)	ROUGE-2 (F1)
1	0.86066	0.29007	0.37307
2	**0.86195**	0.29160	0.37457
3	0.86176	0.29140	0.37442
4	0.86160	**0.29198**	**0.37527**

In order to estimate the model quality, we are using standard precision together with ROUGE-1 & ROUGE-2 metrics. Evaluation metrics for all the aforementioned variations are reported in Table 1 and Table 2. These results show that in most cases setup #4, i.e. sentence nodes with target aspect node and emphasis, gives the best results. It shows that inclusion of topical information helps to get decent quality of summarization. Due to the fact, that most of the competing summarization approaches do not take into account topicality of texts, we do not provide comparisons with them, leaving the creation of fair evaluation setup for the future work.

6 Conclusion

We introduce a biased LexRank model enhanced with the information about topics present in the text. Experiments show that inclusion of topical structure could potentially increase the targeting of the summary and make the overall summarization model benefit from it. However, this research direction requires further exploration and more detailed experimentation.

Acknowledgements. The work of the second author was funded by RFBR, project number 20-37-90025. The work of the last author was funded by RFBR, project number 19-37-60027.

A Appendix

A.1 Experiments with BigARTM and WikiPersons

BigARTM [7, 20] is an open source project for topic modeling of large collections. It allows to train various topic models including multimodal, hierarchical, temporal additively regularized variants. Several experiments on Wikipedia corpus show that BigARTM performs faster and gives better perplexity comparing to other popular packages, such as Vowpal Wabbit and Gensim.

The topic model was trained with the following parameters:

- number of most frequently used words in the text corpora to be included into the dictionary: 2000;
- number of topics: 50;
- weight coefficient for SmoothSparsePhiRegularizer: -2;
- weight coefficient for DecorrelatorPhiRegularizer: 0.00001;
- number of collection passes during the training: 35.

We also conducted the series of experiments varying the parameter d (damping factor), testing the overall model performance on CNN/Daily Mail dataset (Table 3):

Table 3. Topical extractive summarization quality with additively regularized topic model and various d (damping factor) tested on CNN/Daily Mail dataset.

Num	d	F1-score	Recall	Precision
1	0	0.3109	0.5681	0.2254
2	0.1	0.3112	0.5681	0.2258
3	0.2	0.3112	0.5630	0.2267
4	0.3	0.3107	0.5536	0.2283
5	0.4	0.3102	0.5426	0.2302
6	0.5	0.3093	0.5298	0.2322
7	0.6	0.3085	0.5163	0.2347
8	0.7	0.3069	0.5020	0.2364
9	0.8	0.3057	0.4885	0.2388
10	0.9	0.3044	0.4757	0.2410
11	1	0.3027	0.4637	0.2426

A.2   Experiments with Neural Topic Models and WikiPersons

Neural topic models (NTM) provide an optimizable coherence awareness from a text corpora. NTM uses neural variational inference, while basic models such as LDA relies on Gibbs sampling and Bayesian variational inference which appear to be mathematically cumbersome and should be re-derivated even after a small change of modeling assumptions. In our experiments we considered following neural topic models:

- NVDM-GSM [12]. The architecture of the model is a simple VAE [9], which takes the BOW (bag of words) of a document as an input. The topic vector is sampled from the distribution $Q(z|x)$ and then normalized using softmax function (for more details please refer to Fig. 3, which is taken from the Github repo "Neural Topic Models" [24]).

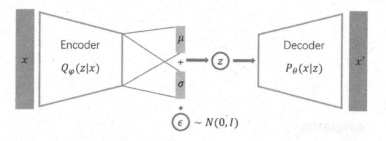

Fig. 3. NVDM-GSM architecture

– ETM [4]. The architecture is a straightforward VAE [9], with the topic-word distribution matrix decomposed as the product of the matrix with topic vectors and the matrix with word vectors (Fig. 4). This model improves the interpretability of topics by locating the topic vectors and the word vectors in the same vector space.

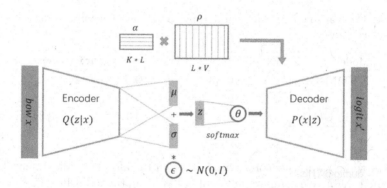

Fig. 4. ETM architecture

– WTM-GMM. An improved model of the WLDA (Weak supervised LDA). Architecturally it is a Wasserstein Auto-Encoder (WAE) [?], that takes Gaussian mixture distribution as a prior distribution and uses Gaussian softmax. The number of components in the Gaussian mixture is usually the same as the number of topics in the model. A detailed scheme of WTM-GMM is presented in Fig. 5 (the picture is taken from the Github repo "Neural Topic Models" [24]).

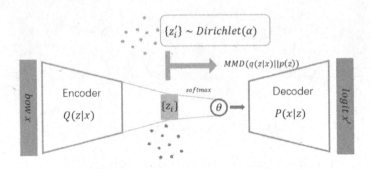

Fig. 5. WTM-GMM architecture

All model implementations were taken from the Neural Topic Models repo[1]. For all the models we set number of topics to 300 and batch size to 512. NVDM-GSM and WTM-GMM were trained for 150 epochs, while ETM was trained for 160 epochs.

Table 4. Comparison between neural topic models (no heterogeneous graph) on WikiPersons dataset

Model	KL div	Topics diversity	c_v	c_uci	c_npmi
NVDM-GSM	**8.15**	**0.83**	**0.45**	**−8.04**	**−0.25**
ETM	3.78	0.54	0.55	−10.47	−0.37
WTM-GMM	-	0.59	0.51	−10.15	−0.34

We provide qualitative comparison between the aforementioned neural topic models in Table 4. We compare different NTM using the following criteria (these metrics are taken from the Coherence model from the library Gensim [17]):

- c_v measure is based on a sliding window, one-set segmentation of the top words and an indirect confirmation measure that uses normalized pointwise mutual information (NPMI) and the cosine similarity
- c_uci measure is based on a sliding window and the pointwise mutual information (PMI) of all word pairs of the given top words:
- c_npmi is an enhanced version of the c_uci coherence using the normalized pointwise mutual information (NPMI).

According to the Table 4 and also manual evaluation of topics by its top tokens, NVDM-GSM model performs better than all the other mentioned models.

Other experimentation included varying the parameter d. However, the average precision increased from 0.643 only to 0.65 with the growth of the damping value.

---

[1] https://github.com/zll17/Neural_Topic_Models.

References

1. Belwal, R.C., Rai, S., Gupta, A.: Text summarization using topic-based vector space model and semantic measure. Inf. Process. Manag. **58**(3), 102536 (2021)
2. Chung, J., Gulcehre, C., Cho, K., Bengio, Y.: Empirical evaluation of gated recurrent neural networks on sequence modeling. arXiv preprint arXiv:1412.3555 (2014)
3. Cui, P., Hu, L., Liu, Y.: Enhancing extractive text summarization with topic-aware graph neural networks. arXiv preprint arXiv:2010.06253 (2020)
4. Dieng, A.B., Ruiz, F.J., Blei, D.M.: Topic modeling in embedding spaces. Trans. Assoc. Comput. Linguist. **8**, 439–453 (2020)
5. Erkan, G.: Using biased random walks for focused summarization (2006)
6. He, R., Lee, W.S., Ng, H.T., Dahlmeier, D.: An unsupervised neural attention model for aspect extraction. In: Proceedings of the 55th Annual Meeting of the Association for Computational Linguistics (Volume 1: Long Papers), Vancouver, Canada, pp. 388–397. Association for Computational Linguistics, July 2017. https://doi.org/10.18653/v1/P17-1036. https://www.aclweb.org/anthology/P17-1036
7. Ianina, A., Vorontsov, K.: Multimodal topic modeling for exploratory search in collective blog. J. Mach. Learn. Data Anal. **2**(2), 173–186 (2016)
8. Iyyer, M., Guha, A., Chaturvedi, S., Boyd-Graber, J., Daumé III, H.: Feuding families and former friends: unsupervised learning for dynamic fictional relationships. In: Proceedings of the 2016 Conference of the North American Chapter of the Association for Computational Linguistics: Human Language Technologies, pp. 1534–1544 (2016)
9. Kingma, D.P., Welling, M.: Auto-encoding variational Bayes. arXiv preprint arXiv:1312.6114 (2013)
10. Kipf, T.N., Welling, M.: Semi-supervised classification with graph convolutional networks. arXiv preprint arXiv:1609.02907 (2016)
11. Lin, C.Y., Och, F.: Looking for a few good metrics: rouge and its evaluation. In: NTCIR Workshop (2004)
12. Miao, Y., Grefenstette, E., Blunsom, P.: Discovering discrete latent topics with neural variational inference. arXiv preprint arXiv:1706.00359 (2017)
13. Miao, Y., Yu, L., Blunsom, P.: Neural variational inference for text processing. In: International Conference on Machine Learning, pp. 1727–1736 (2016)
14. Mihalcea, R., Tarau, P.: TextRank: bringing order into text. In: Proceedings of the 2004 Conference on Empirical Methods in Natural Language Processing, Barcelona, Spain, pp. 404–411. Association for Computational Linguistics, July 2004. https://www.aclweb.org/anthology/W04-3252
15. Nallapati, R., Zhai, F., Zhou, B.: SummaRuNNer: a recurrent neural network based sequence model for extractive summarization of documents (2016)
16. Otterbacher, J., Erkan, G., Radev, D.R.: Biased LexRank: passage retrieval using random walks with question-based priors. Inf. Process. Manag. **45**(1), 42–54 (2009)
17. Rehurek, R., Sojka, P.: Gensim-python framework for vector space modelling. NLP Centre, Faculty of Informatics, Masaryk University, Brno, Czech Republic, vol. 3, no. 2 (2011)
18. Socher, R., Karpathy, A., Le, Q.V., Manning, C.D., Ng, A.Y.: Grounded compositional semantics for finding and describing images with sentences. Trans. Assoc. Comput. Linguist. **2**, 207–218 (2014)

19. Vorontsov, K., Frei, O., Apishev, M., Romov, P., Dudarenko, M.: BigARTM: open source library for regularized multimodal topic modeling of large collections. In: Khachay, M.Y., Konstantinova, N., Panchenko, A., Ignatov, D.I., Labunets, V.G. (eds.) AIST 2015. CCIS, vol. 542, pp. 370–381. Springer, Cham (2015). https://doi.org/10.1007/978-3-319-26123-2_36

20. Vorontsov, K., Frei, O., Apishev, M., Romov, P., Suvorova, M., Yanina, A.: Non-Bayesian additive regularization for multimodal topic modeling of large collections. In: Proceedings of the 2015 Workshop on Topic Models: Post-processing and Applications, pp. 29–37 (2015)

21. Weston, J., Bengio, S., Usunier, N.: WSABIE: scaling up to large vocabulary image annotation. In: Twenty-Second International Joint Conference on Artificial Intelligence (2011)

22. Xu, J., Gan, Z., Cheng, Y., Liu, J.: Discourse-aware neural extractive text summarization (2020)

23. Yasunaga, M., Zhang, R., Meelu, K., Pareek, A., Srinivasan, K., Radev, D.: Graph-based neural multi-document summarization. In: Proceedings of the 21st Conference on Computational Natural Language Learning (CoNLL 2017), Vancouver, Canada, pp. 452–462. Association for Computational Linguistics, August 2017. https://doi.org/10.18653/v1/K17-1045. https://www.aclweb.org/anthology/K17-1045

24. Zhang, L.: Neural topic models (2020). https://github.com/zll17/Neural_Topic_Models

25. Zhu, H., Dong, L., Wei, F., Qin, B., Liu, T.: Transforming wikipedia into augmented data for query-focused summarization (2019)

The Semantic Shifts of the Topical Structure in the Corpus of Lentach News Posts

Ivan D. Mamaev[1,2]([✉]) [iD], Alena A. Mamaeva[3] [iD], and Daria A. Axenova[1] [iD]

[1] Baltic State Technical University "Voenmeh" named after D.F. Ustinov, 1-ya Krasnoarmeyskaya Street, 1, 190005 Saint Petersburg, Russia
{mamaev_id,aksenova_da}@voenmeh.ru
[2] Faculty of Philology, Saint Petersburg State University, Universitetskaya Embankment 11, 199034 Saint Petersburg, Russia
[3] ITMO University, Saint Petersburg State University, Kronversky Avenue, 49, 197101 Saint Petersburg, Russia
az998@mail.ru

Abstract. Nowadays the interests of linguists are aimed at analyzing text collections with the help of automatic procedures. They pay special attention to the texts on social networks as their language features differ from the features of fiction texts or scientific articles. The paper is dedicated to the creation of dynamic topic models of Lentach news posts on VK social network. We use a mixture of NLP libraries to identify the semantic shifts of main topical sets since the end of 2018. The corpus contains more than 26,000 posts on various topics. In contemporary Russian linguistic papers, the collection of Lentach posts is rarely analyzed in terms of NLP. The results show that the main topics that are widely discussed in this community cover sports events, health issues, and protests.

Keywords: Russian · Corpus linguistics · Social networks · Dynamic topic models · Semantics

1 Introduction

In recent decades, with the development of the Web, the qualities and accessibility of different shapes of media have essentially expanded: online magazines, music, podcasts, news communities, etc. The media might have an impact on people of different ages, especially teenagers as they are still perceiving key social norms and roles and forming their own identities. That's why contemporary analysts center on the investigation of media sources from original points of view.

Nowadays social media news posts are becoming one of the most consumed forms of media. With the help of up-to-date tools, linguists can track the development of the media language on the Internet. Recent linguistic studies [6, 15] show that it has become popular to use different approaches to topic modeling. One of such algorithms is known as dynamic topic modeling (DTM) that allows scientists to track semantics changes of posts over time.

V. Malykh and A. Filchenkov (Eds.): AINL 2022, CCIS 1731, pp. 27–39, 2022.
https://doi.org/10.1007/978-3-031-23372-2_3

We decided to analyze the dynamic structure of Lentach news posts topics for some reasons. First of all, researchers study both the news content itself [15] and individual components of the community (for example, the representation of brands [1]). Secondly, the editors of this community can informally present almost any news to readers. Moreover, Lentach posts are seldom analyzed from the point of view of natural language processing. Finally, the linguistic properties of news on social networks differ from the linguistic properties of news in conventional media. We chose posts from the end of 2018 till the beginning of 2022 as the period was full of different pivotal events both for the world and the Russian Federation: Ukranian presidential elections in 2019 and American ones in 2020, Belarussian protests in 2020, coronavirus pandemic, etc.

2   Related Works

Topic modeling procedures were primarily developed for processing a large amount of data, nowadays they are used in various disciplines. For instance, [9] discusses such a field of Germany's politics as coal legislation. The authors apply dynamic topic modeling for analyzing more than 800,000 parliamentary speeches (1949–2019). It turned out that in the 1950s coal was a driver of economic prosperity in Germany, that's why it was estimated positively. In the 2010s, there were more debates organized by the Greens and the Left Party, they were held in the context of climate protection. As the result, the debates had negative sentiments.

Another field, that is actively discussed, is engineering sciences. The paper [4] is devoted to the study of topical evolvement in radar technology papers. The authors used LDA-modified dynamic topic modeling for Scopus articles that were published before the beginning of 2019. The resultant 108 topics were divided into two categories: radar development and radar application. Here are some of the topical popularities: the *monopulse radar* topic was a hot one until 1971, the *weather radar* topic was actively discussed between 1978 and 1984, and the *radar monitoring of meteorological disasters* topic was acute between 1981 and 2006.

Linguistics is also subject to analysis with the help of modern machine learning methods. In recent years, we faced a new discipline titled computational sociolinguistics. Its main goal is to study the connection of the society and the language with the help of some computational methods [10]. The paper [17] contributes to the discussion of the interplay between the *Englishnization* process and organizational culture. A detailed analysis of the dynamic topics of the *Englishnization* process reveals a pressing issue facing Japanese multinational companies concerning the balance of multinational cohesion with monolingualism and multiculturalism.

All the papers mentioned above are based on English text collections. At the same time, it is important to mention that dynamic topic modeling approaches can be applied to Russian corpora. Within recent years Russian scholars pay attention to the topical analysis of Russian governmental messages from social media. In [13, 14], the authors use three different topic modeling algorithms (Latent Semantic Indexing (LSI), Latent Dirichlet Allocation (LDA), and Dynamic Topic Modeling (DTM) with non-negative matrix factorization) to detect topics in the texts of RBK Group and governmental websites. The results of DTM with non-negative matrix factorization were as precise as the results of LSI and LDA algorithms were, moreover, DTM required less time for processing texts.

Semantic topics of literary texts were described in [11]. The authors apply LDA to four poetry corpora (1600–1925): Russian, Czech, German, and English. For instance, the *Sea* topic is most acute for both Russian and German periods of Romanticism. It has a rising tendency in the second half of the XIX century and stays stable within modern times. As for the *Stars* topic, it arose in the Russian Late Romanticism (1825–1850). Another paper [16] discusses some niche topics in Russian prose of the first third of the XX century that were detected with the help of DTM with non-negative matrix factorization. They describe the main events in the history of both Imperial Russia and Soviet Russia: revolutions, philosopher's ships, etc.

The current paper is going to continue the studies in the analysis of the dynamic semantic structure of Russian texts.

3 Experimental Design

3.1 Corpus Collecting and Preprocessing

The development of the corpus of Lentach news posts began with the choice of a period. At the moment of running the experiments, the first post of Lentach community on VKontakte social network was published on March 19, 2014. In March 2014, the Crimea became a part of the Russian Federation, and the process of transferring the peninsula to Russia was widely covered in the press. The first Lentach posts were also devoted to the Crimean problems. Nonetheless, we decided not to analyze all the community posts. We chose the posts that had been published since the end of 2018. In this case, we were able to divide the corpus into posts of two periods: a pre-pandemic period and a pandemic one. The time length of each period is approximately one and a half years. Thus, we were able to trace whether there had been any quantitative or qualitative changes in the semantic structure of news and how the coronavirus had affected the topical distribution of news texts.

The parser for collecting news posts was developed for Python 3.7[1] and maintained with requests[2] and vk_api[3] libraries. During collecting posts, we had to exclude non-textual elements: emoticons, pictures, videos, etc. It was important to save the time of publishing a post in the following format: *YYYY-MM-DD (YYYY – years, MM – months, DD – days)*. The resultant number of posts turned out to be more than 26,000.

The next step was corpus processing which included tokenization, lemmatization, and stop-words removal. The procedure was performed by means of Stanza[4] library. It can be a beneficial alternative for other widely-used NLP toolkits. The library is easily adapted to texts of different genres, and the results of state-of-the-art performance will stay at a high level compared to the existed libraries [12]. During lemmatization, each word was checked for its presence in the stop-list which includes prepositions,

---

[1] https://www.python.org/downloads/release/python-370/.
[2] https://docs.python-requests.org/en/latest/.
[3] https://vk-api.readthedocs.io/en/latest/.
[4] https://stanfordnlp.github.io/stanza/.

conjunctions, particles, obscene vocabulary, abbreviations, etc. The total number of stop words was more than 1400, and it was compiled with the help of the Russian National Corpus[5] and a Frequency Dictionary of Contemporary Russian by O.N. Lyashevskaya and S.A. Sharov[6]. These resources proved their efficiency in filtering social media texts [7, 8]. After preprocessing, the size of the corpus was more than 600,000 tokens.

3.2 BERT Topic Modeling

The first algorithms of topic models were based on algebraic transformations like LSI. Later algebraic models were replaced with probabilistic topic models like LDA or Probabilistic Latent Semantic Analysis (PLSA). These procedures allow one to extract meaningful topical sets of words from both structured and unstructured texts [2]. Unfortunately, such models cannot take context into account, that is why some semantic features of topical sets are likely to be omitted. Nowadays, pre-trained language models like BERT fill in this gap, they are used in numerous NLP applications, and topic modeling is not an exception. One of such implementations is BERTopic. It is an approach that uses transformers and c-TF-IDF and creates dense clusters for interpretable topics, it allows keeping important words in the topic descriptions[7].

To perform dynamic BERT topic modeling with the help of BERTopic, we first needed to create a basic topic model using all the news posts. To obtain it, we used the *BERTopic()* function. We also visualized the basic topics that were created using the Intertopic Distance Map. This allowed us to understand whether the basic topics are sufficient. If they are sufficient, we can proceed with creating dynamic topics (Fig. 1).

There are more than 200 topics in Fig. 1, some of them overlap each other. Overlapping means that visualized topics are in the same semantic field and they might show us the evolvement of this field. At the same time, the smaller topic is, the less meaningful it is for tracking the development. To reduce the number of unnecessary topics, it was decided to tune the model up with the help of the *min_topic_size* parameter. The parameter is used to specify the minimum size of a topic. The default value is equal to 10, so it was necessary to set it higher. After running several experiments, we found out that the optimal value of the *min_topic_size* parameter for Lentach posts is equal to 60 (Fig. 2).

We can see that less important topical sets were not taken into consideration, the total number of topics is 58. After tuning up we were able to start creating the dynamic structure of topic models. There were some important parameters that one should take note of. First of all, the *docs* parameter contained all the posts we are using. The *topics* parameter contained the topics we had just created. Finally, the *timestamps* parameter contained the time information of each post. Finally, the following plot was obtained (Fig. 3).

The vertical axis shows the number of occurrences of a particular topic in a certain number of posts, the horizontal axis shows the time of publishing posts. It is difficult to perform any further analysis with such a huge number of visualized topics, so in the following sections, we will focus on the dynamics of separate topics.

---

[5] https://ruscorpora.ru/new/.

[6] http://dict.ruslang.ru/freq.php.

[7] https://github.com/MaartenGr/BERTopic.

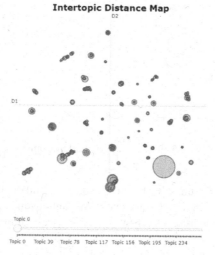

Fig. 1. The distribution of basic topics before tuning up

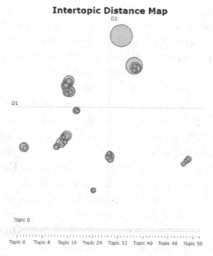

Fig. 2. The distribution of basic topics after tuning up

In any DTM, the parameter of chronological periods can be of two different types. In the first case, we simply set the time step and look at some changes. As a result, topic models reflect the dynamics of topics without references to events in the world, we observe just the dynamics of topics over time. In the second case, we can indicate time intervals not from a formal point of view, but from a meaningful one. For example, when analyzing literary works, we can highlight major milestones: the 1850s, 1900s, 1950s, and so on. With this approach, we will be able to see the connection between social processes and the changes of topics in the texts. To sum it up, the time parameter can be meaningful (informative topic models) and formal (simplification of the topic models

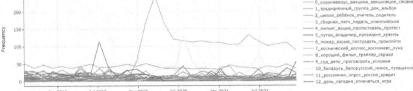

Fig. 3. The evolution of all the topics

analysis procedure). Unfortunately, the media space and media texts have been formed as a whole recently compared to literary texts. We cannot single out informative topical patterns because of this feature, as a result of which we will turn to formal periods of time.

4 Results and Interpretation

The first brief analysis conveys the suggestion that the pre-pandemic period (till March 2020) was characterized by a relatively homogeneous evolvement of the topical structure. Also, when analyzing the frequency distribution of topics, we can say that during the coronavirus pandemic, the news community began to publish more posts on certain topics. One of the most frequent topics is the *health* topic. It is important to note that despite the set of topical words presented in Fig. 3 (topical index is 0, an orange line), we argue that the topic is dedicated specifically to health issues, so the first lemma of the set cannot be a topic label. Upon closer analysis, it turns out that at the beginning of 2020 there was a semantic shift in the topic, as in the pre-pandemic period, the news community published posts on other common diseases: HIV, chickenpox, bubonic plague, hepatitis, etc. In traditional linguistics, a *semantic shift (drift)* refers to a change in the lexical meaning of a word that is observed as a difference in the meaning of the same word in different historical periods of language development [3]. In the current study, we define a *semantic shift* as a change in lexical units in dynamic topic models. As a result of the changes, more general topical concepts are narrowed to more specific ones at a certain period. This shift happens with a sharp increase in the number of analyzed texts. In other words, such shifts are frequency peaks that detect pivotal news agenda. In this section, we describe the main examples of semantic shifts of some topics.

In Fig. 4, we can see that the spring period of 2019 was characterized with such paradigmatically and syntagmatically close words as *chickenpox, hiv, hepatitis, vaccination (ветрянка, вич, гепатит, вакцинопрофилактика),* etc. Here is one of the health posts published in March 2019[8]: *Thanks to decades of successful vaccination, we rarely hear about tetanus. Nonetheless, the danger of this disease will never disappear, thousands of people die from it every year… (Благодаря десятилетиям успешной вакцинопрофилактики мы нечасто слышим о столбняке. Тем не менее,*

---

[8] https://vk.com/lentach?w=wall-29534144_10799081.

опасность этой болезни никогда не исчезнет, ежегодно от неё умирают тысячи людей...). The structure remains quite stable without any significant frequency peaks until March 2020.

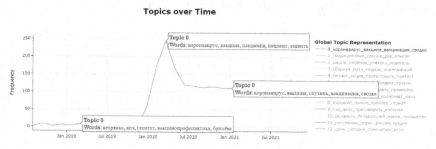

Fig. 4. The evolution of the *health* topic

While the *health* topic remains relevant to this day, it is pivotal to note other topics that have been covered in detail by media over the past few years. One of them the *protests and strikes* topic (cf. Figure 3, topical index is 4, a red line). In contrast to the unimodal distribution of the health topic, we see that the frequency distribution of this topic is multimodal. The multimodal distribution shows that the observed sample of posts is not homogeneous. In other words, there were at least three events that led to a semantic shift from the general topic of protests and strikes to more specific ones. Figure 5 shows the distribution, in which the following periods can be clearly distinguished: July 2019, July and August 2020, and January 2021.

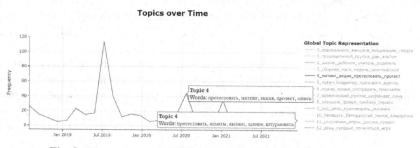

Fig. 5. The multimodal distribution of the *protests and strikes* topic

The first period describes so-called summer protests. Thousands of authorized and unauthorized protest actions in Moscow began in the middle of 2019, the situation escalated around the elections to the Moscow City Duma. As part of the preparations for the elections, independent candidates from the non-systemic opposition announced numerous violations by the authorities, election committees, and their political opponents during the registration of candidates.

The second period describes the protests that began after the election of the President of Belarus in 2020. These protests took on a nationwide scale, and the situation in the country began to be characterized as a political crisis. This period is characterized by the following set of lemmata: *rebel, protest, action, protest, minsk (протестовать, митинг, акция, протест, минск)*, etc. This dynamic sub-topic of the protests is also reflected in topic 10, which is entirely dedicated to Belarus. In this topic, the only activity of publishing posts is observed in the same period (Fig. 6).

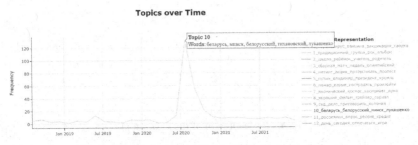

Fig. 6. The evolvement of topic 10 dedicated to *Belarus*

Finally, the third peak refers to news posts that describe protests in support of Russian opposition leader Alexei Navalny. These protests began in January 2021 after publishing an investigative documentary about the President of the Russian Federation and detaining Navalny upon his return to Russia from Germany. Protest actions were held in many Russian cities.

Since the experiment was conducted at the beginning of 2022, we can notice an increase in the number of posts dedicated to protests in the tail of the distribution. There is a tendency to the fourth semantic shift of the *protests and strikes* topic: *protest, almaty, akimat, building, storm (протестовать, алматы, акимат, здание, штурмовать)*, etc. This set of words describes the January waves of protests in Kazakhstan after a sharp increase in liquefied gas prices. The protests turned into riots and clashes with the security forces.

Earlier we mentioned that the topic of protests was linked with elections and voting. Since several important election processes have taken place both in Russia and the world since the end of 2019, the topic of *elections* was also reflected in the resultant topic model (topical index is 15, a blue line).

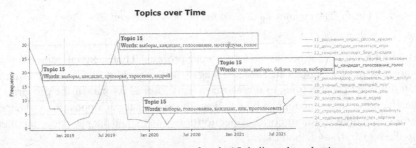

Fig. 7. The evolvement of topic 15 dedicated to *elections*

The distribution shown in Fig. 7 has two peaks, the left tail tends to decrease and the right one tends to rise. The decrease in the left tail is due to a decrease in the number of posts on the topic of the governmental elections at the end of 2018. In particular, the set of topical words *elections, candidate, primorye, tarasenko* (*выборы, кандидат, приморье, тарасенко*) focuses on the electoral situation in Primorsky Krai. The first peak characterizes the elections to the Moscow City Duma. The second topical peak is associated with the active publication of news posts, which describe the presidential race of Biden and Trump. Finally, the increase in the right tail of the distribution is directly related to the news about the autumn elections to the State Duma in 2021.

Also, among the variety of dynamic structures obtained, we can emphasize the *sports* topic (topical index is 3, a yellow line). Figure 8 shows the change in the topical set of words.

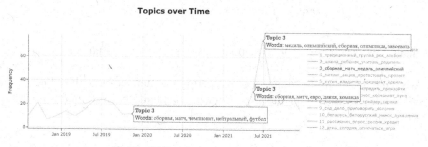

Fig. 8. The evolvement of the *sports* topic

During relatively stable intervals, the editors of Lentach community published sports news dedicated to individual events (for instance, a football or hockey match, boxing, etc.). During the summer of 2021, there was a significant increase in sports news publishing due to two events. First of all, the 2020 UEFA European Football Championship was held in the first half of the summer of 2021. The event was postponed in 2020 because of the coronavirus pandemic. A notable example of the event is that one of the dynamic sub-topics is characterized by such words as *national team, match, euro, denmark, team* (*сборная, матч, евро, дания, команда*), etc. In the second half of the summer of 2021, the media paid detailed attention to the Tokyo Olympics. The distribution peak is described by such words as *medal, olympic, national team, olympics, win* (*медаль, олимпийский, сборная, олимпиада, завоевать*), etc.

Among the analyzed topic models, we can highlight those that develop more evenly and without any special semantic changes. This homogeneity has two special features. Firstly, we do not observe a sharp increase in texts on this topic, their number remains approximately at the same quantitative level. Secondly, a particular topic runs like a red thread through the entire history of mankind, which will be constantly reflected in the texts and resultant topic models. For instance, topic 39 is devoted to death. It should be noted that within one sub-topic, some news about the death of different people can be combined. In Fig. 9, the left sub-topic is characterized by such words as *die, actor, buldakov, kovalsky (смерть, актёр, булдаков, ковальский),* etc. Editor-in-chief of Kommersant-Vlast Maxim Kovalsky and Russian actor Vladimir Buldakov died approximately at the same time: March 29, 2019, and April 3, 2019.

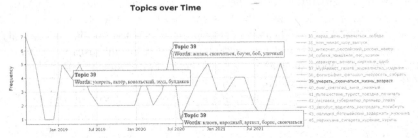

Fig. 9. The evolvement of the *death* topic

Finally, we can highlight topics that start developing only at certain time intervals due to natural reasons. Topic 40 is dedicated to *winter issues*: snow removal, roof cleaning, etc. We see that within the majority of the period the number of analyzed news tends to be 0, while in winter the editors of Lentach community begin to publish news that describes winter issues (Fig. 10).

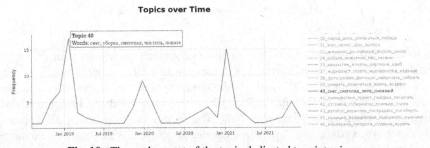

Fig. 10. The evolvement of the topic dedicated to *winter issues*

5 Discussion

As a result of the analysis of the obtained semantic and topical structure of posts, we can distinguish three main groups of topics. The first group is a group in which the semantic shifts of topics are heterogeneous. The time intervals between peaks vary greatly, and the number of documents analyzed during these peaks also varies greatly. For example, such topics are a *health* topic or a *sports* one. The second group is characterized by the homogeneity of semantic shifts over time and the number of documents. One of the reasons for the homogeneous distribution may be a natural coincidence: for example, the topic of *winter issues*. Finally, the last group does not have strongly marked semantic shifts, which indicates an even development of a topic. In Sect. 4, we characterized the topic of *death*.

While creating contextualized dynamic topic models, we can notice some advantages. First of all, different topic modeling procedures (LDA, DTM with NMF, etc.) have already been successfully adapted to Russian corpora of posts on social networks [5, 7]. With fine-tuned text preprocessing there are almost no quaint or uninterpretable topical sets. From the graphical point of view, the texts of news are unlikely to consist of any specific signs, even if they are published on social networks. Unlike the personal texts of users, news texts are more stable. Moreover, BERTopic contains all the necessary visualization components so that one would not use a combination of different libraries. For instance, visualizing of the standard LDA topics in the gensim[9] library can be carried out only using pyLDAvis[10]. Sometimes it can be inconvenient. Finally, like in the standard LDA, BERTopic also allows to track some syntagmatic and paradigmatic relations among words. For instance, in Fig. 10, there are derivational relations between the *snow (снег)* word and the *snowfall (снегопад)* word.

At the same time, we can highlight some difficulties we faced during the experiment. It is impossible to obtain a list of dynamic topics that change over time. One can only see them in the resultant figures. Another pivotal feature of the current study is the absence of the automatic labeling of topics. In the current study, all the topics were named manually. There are some automatic ways to obtain a topic label. One can use external sources (search engines or vector models of any corpus) or internal sources (the hashtags of analyzed posts) [7, 8].

Finally, it is worth noting that our conclusions related to the performance of preprocessing and topic modeling are based on the single dataset, so all conclusions might not generalize to different textual genres in the Russian language and corpora. It is seen that optimal preprocessing procedures and the selection of proper topic modeling algorithms depend strongly on the data.

6 Summary

The study has demonstrated that in spite of the variety of news posts contextualized topic modeling can distinguish diverse semantic and topical structures. We were also able to make sure that the concept of a semantic shift in topical sets of words largely depends on the external situation in the world. The first half of the common chart with all the extracted topics has evolved more evenly than the second half since March 2020. The coronavirus has affected many life areas, as a result of which the expected shifts did not occur in 2020, but in 2021 after the world had adapted to new realities.

This experiment was carried out on a limited amount of data, but the approach itself can be applied in a real-time environment in many scientific domains. In linguistics, this method can be used in modern corpus tools to create actual topical dynamics of corpus texts of different genres. In politics, dynamic topic modeling can be a useful tool for detecting social problems and policy-making.

---

[9] https://radimrehurek.com/gensim/.
[10] https://pyldavis.readthedocs.io/en/latest/readme.html.

Of course, the research can be continued in some directions. First, statistical topic modeling and contextualized topic modeling can be combined for identifying specific features of the dataset. Secondly, the resultant topical sets can be marked up both automatically using external and internal sources, and manually using annotators. Finally, for a more detailed study of news in social media, our corpus can be extended with posts from other news communities.

References

1. Antropova, V.: Brand representation in news communities (based on Lentach Community) (Predstavlenie brendov v novostnyh soobshchestvah socsetej (na primere gruppy "Lentach")). In: Branding as a communicative technology of the XXI century (Brending kak kommunikativnaya tekhnologiya XXI veka), pp. 22–26 (2019)
2. Bianchi, F., Terragni, S., Hovy, D., Nozza, D., Fersini, E.: Cross-lingual contextualized topic models with zero-shot learning. In: arXiv preprint arXiv:2004.07737 (2020)
3. Blank, A.: Why do new meanings occur? a cognitive typology of the motivations for lexical semantic change andreas blank. In: Cognitive Linguistics Research, pp. 61–89 (1999)
4. Huang, X., Fang, H.: Topic evolution analysis of radar research using a dynamic topic model based on latent Dirichlet allocation. In: Journal of Physics: Conference Series, vol. 2010, No. 1. IOP Publishing (2021)
5. Koltsov, S., Pashakhin, S., Dokuka, S.: A full-cycle methodology for news topic modeling and user feedback research. In: Staab, S., Koltsova, O., Ignatov, D.I. (eds.) SocInfo 2018. LNCS, vol. 11185, pp. 308–321. Springer, Cham (2018)
6. Maltseva, A., Shilkina, N., Evseev, E., Matveev, M., Makhnytkina, O.: Topic modeling of russian-language texts using the parts-of-speech composition of topics (on the example of volunteer movement semantics in social media). In: 2021 29th Conference of Open Innovations Association (FRUCT), pp. 247–253. IEEE (2021)
7. Mamaev, I., Mitrofanova, O.: Automatic detection of hidden communities in the texts of russian social network corpus. In: Filchenkov, A., Kauttonen, J., Pivovarova, L. (eds.) AINL 2020. CCIS, vol. 1292, pp. 17–33. Springer, Cham (2020). https://doi.org/10.1007/978-3-030-59082-6_2
8. Mitrofanova, O., Sampetova, V., Mamaev, I., Moskvina, A., Sukharev, K.: Topic modelling of the russian corpus of pikabu posts: author-topic distribution and topic labelling. In: International Conference "Internet and Modern Society" (IMS-2020). CEUR Proceedings, pp. 101–116 (2020)
9. Müller-Hansen, F., Callaghan, M.W., Lee, Y.T., Leipprand, A., Flachsland, C., Minx, J.C.: Who cares about coal? analyzing 70 years of German parliamentary debates on coal with dynamic topic modeling. Energy Res. Soci. Sci. **72** (2021)
10. Nguyen, D., Doğruöz, A.S., Rosé, C.P., De Jong, F.: Computational sociolinguistics: a survey. Comput. Linguist. **42**(3), 537–593 (2016)
11. Plechac, P., Haider, T.N.: Mapping topic evolution across poetic traditions. In: arXiv preprint arXiv:2006.15732 (2020)
12. Qi, P., Zhang, Y., Zhang, Y., Bolton, J., Manning, C.D.: Stanza: a python natural language processing toolkit for many human languages. In: arXiv preprint arXiv:2003.07082 (2020)
13. Skitalinskaya, G., Aleksandrov, M., Danilova, V., Stefanovsky, D.: Website materials of governmental and regional administrations of Russia in terms of dynamic topic modeling (Materialy saytov pravitel'stva i regional'nykh administraciy Rossii v zerkale dinamicheskogo tematicheskogo modelirovaniya). In: Mathematical Modeling of Social Processes (Matematicheskoe Modelirovanie Social'nykh Processov), vol. 20, 166–174 (2018)

14. Skitalinskaya, G.: Analysis of news dynamics using two-step dynamic topic modeling algorithms (Analiz dinamiki novostey s pomoshch'yu dvukh-shagovykh algoritmov dinamicheskogo tematicheskogo modelirovaniya). In: Mathematical Modeling of Social Processes (Matematicheskoe Modelirovanie Social'nykh Processov), vol. 19, 97–104 (2017)
15. Spevak, D., Zholnerovich, P.: A comparative analysis of lentach public and tea with raspberry jam public on VK social network (Sravnitel'nyj analiz pablikov «Lentach» i «Chaj z malinavym varennem» v social'noy seti VKontakte). In: The Volzhsky Scientific Journal (Volzhsky Vestnik Nauki), pp. 23–26 (2016)
16. Zamiraylova, E., Mitrofanova, O.: Dynamic topic modeling of Russian prose of the first third of the XXth century by means of non-negative matrix factorization. In: Proceedings of the III International Conference on Language Engineering and Applied Linguistics (PRLEAL-2019), CEUR Workshop Proceedings, vol. 2552, pp. 321–339 (2020)
17. Zhang, Z.: Analyzing cultural expatriates' attitudes toward "Englishnization" using dynamic topic modeling. J. Comput.-Assist. Ling. Res. 5(1), 1–26 (2021)

Development of Folklore Motif Classifier Using Limited Data

Maria Matveeva[1]([✉]) and Valentin Malykh[2]

[1] Novosibirsk State University, Novosibirsk, Russia
m.matveeva@g.nsu.ru \
[2] Kazan Federal University, Kazan, Russia

Abstract. The existence of mythological universals - common or similar folklore images and motifs in different cultures, makes it possible to catalog them and present them in the form of classifications. Attributing folklore texts to certain motifs is part of the work of folklorists, but at the moment only manual marking is possible. This paper proposes methods for developing a classifier of folklore motifs using the zero-shot approach, which makes it possible to train the classifier on a limited dataset, and also allows to predict the motif for any text, even if the text with such a motif was not present in the training set. Various ways of vectorizing texts and various models were tested. Evaluation of the results of the classifiers' work allows us to assert that the developed classifier can correlate texts with motifs with sufficient accuracy.

Keywords: Text classification · Zero-shot learning · Multi-label classification

1 Introduction

Folktales are the cultural universals found in all human communities from prehistoric times to the present. Not only the idea of the folktale itself is universal - many plots and their elements are found simultaneously in many cultures. Because of this, there is a need for cataloging folklore material: such catalogs allow researchers to navigate in a large number of texts. The most widely used catalog of folklore stories is the Aarne-Thompson-Uther (ATU) index, which consists of more than 2,000 descriptions of various folklore motifs. Its structure is described in more detail in Sect. 3.1.

The problem of labeling texts with motifs is that it takes a lot of time and effort, and also requires labeling expertise in this area. Moreover, manual markup can be prone to errors. Thus, solving the problem of automatic marking of texts according to the ATU index will not only speed up the process of marking up new texts but can also prompt researchers with insights regarding previously marked texts.

The goal of this study was to develop an automatic subject classifier that can assign one or several motifs to a text. In this work, we presented a dataset in

V. Malykh and A. Filchenkov (Eds.): AINL 2022, CCIS 1731, pp. 40–48, 2022.
https://doi.org/10.1007/978-3-031-23372-2_4

tabular form, tried various ways to vectorize texts, and trained three classifying models. As a result, we got metrics that show the efficiency of the approach.

The paper is divided into the following sections: in Sect. 2 a review of the literature on topics similar to the topic of this work. The first part of it is devoted to zero-shot approaches to text processing, the other - to the previous studies of texts, marked according to the ATU index, with the use of NLP approaches. Section 3 describes two components of the dataset that has been used - the ATU index itself and the catalog of folk tales, as well as the rationale why they were chosen for the study. Section 4 describes the general approach that was proposed to solve the problem, taking into account its specificity. Section 5 is devoted to the description of the technical implementation of each part of the text classifier, followed by the results and the conclusion.

2   Related Work

2.1   Zero-Shot Text Classification

The first article about the zero-shot approach for text classification appeared in 2008: the authors applied to the texts Explicit Semantic Analysis, an algorithm that generates a set of concepts that are weighted and ordered by their relevance to the input [4], and used vector representations of such sets and labels for training a naive Bayes classifier [2]. Such a model could predict labels for unseen classes with accuracy compared to those of classified approaches. Pushp and Srivastava suggested various network architectures that are able to learn the relationship between text and weakly labeled tags by training models on a binary classification task, where one available label was correct and another one was random [13]. Zhang et al. used a two-phased network that uses different approaches for seen and unseen classes in a test set [18]. The technique we are using in this paper was inspired by the article 'Learning Transferable Visual Models From Natural Language Supervision' [15], where an image encoder and a text encoder are trained simultaneously to predict the correct pairings of a batch of (image, text) training examples, although in our case both encoders are working with text. The approach will be described in more detail in further sections.

Problems similar to those described in this article can often be found in application to medical texts. For example, the zero-shot approach allows to automate the process of coding clinical records according to ICD - International Classification of Diseases. Firstly, like the Aarne-Thompson index, ICD has a hierarchical structure and every entry consists of an index and some description. Secondly, it is the task of marking up small noisy texts. Song et al. used the combination of zero-shot approach and generative adversarial network trained on ICD labels to extract meaningful features from them [16]. Kong et al. used zero-shot entity retrieval and knowledge graphs to create a system that makes it easier to find information about newly appeared medical conditions and drug treatments which helps medical specialists to improve patient care [5]. Another option for solving the entity retrieval problem is proposed in the article [10], where zero-shot approach and transfer learning were used to extract structured information from pathology reports.

2.2 Working with ATU Index Labeled Texts

Due to a large amount of text marked up with the ATU index, there are many studies using this markup in one way or another. Ofek et al. used sequence mining methods to analyze tales in which each part was marked with a motif, and also introduced a classifier of marked tales [8]. Nakawake and Sato analyzed tales, marked in ATU index as "Animal Tales" to build co-occurrence graphs of wild, domestic animals, and human [7]. D'Huy built a network of relations between tales, marked as "Tales of Magic" in the ATU index [3].

3 Dataset

3.1 ATU Index

In our research, we used Aarne-Thompson-Uther index, a catalog of folktale types widely used to classify and systematize folklore texts. This catalog contains about 2400 motifs presented in a hierarchical structure: the plots are divided into 7 categories according to subgenres. Each plot has a number, a short description, and examples of materials to illustrate the plot. For the experiments, only the number and a short description of the plot were used.

It's important to note that we used its Russian-language version, created by folklorist N.P. Andreyev. This version has the same structure as the original index, but includes some variations of tales specific for Russian culture. Because of this, the total number of motifs described in this index is 2640. Many stories in the Russian-language version are illustrated with folktales from Afanasyev's collection, thus, this catalog is the most suitable for our research.

motif_code	motif_description
1	Лиса крадет рыбу с воза (саней): притворившись мертвой, ложится...
154	Мужик, медведь и лиса: лиса хитрыми советами помогает мужику избавиться...
161A*	Медведь на липовой ноге: приходит в избу старика и старухи за своей...

Fig. 1. Example of the elements of ATU index used in the study: every entry consists of a motif code and a short description of a plot

3.2   Texts

As mentioned above, to create a dataset we scraped and parsed Afanasyev's collection of Russian folk tales manually annotated with the codes according to the Russian version of the Aarne-Thompson index. A total of 415 texts were received. 72% of the texts were marked with one motif, the rest - with several ones (up to 8 motifs).

The dataset with the texts was chosen on the following grounds: the texts of folk tales collected by Afanasyev are one of the largest collections of Russian folk tales ever collected. Also, because of reprints, they can be found published in the modern Russian language, which means that modern pre-trained models such as BERT are applicable to them. The most prominent works concerning Afanasyev's tales are the works of Vladimir Propp [11,12], which had a great influence on the development of folklore studies and structuralism approach in folklore studies (Fig. 2).

title	text	motif
Лисичка-сестричка и волк	Жил себе дед да баба. Дед говорит бабе: «Ты, баба, пеки пироги, а я поеду...	1
Мужик, медведь и лиса	У мужика с медведем была большая дружба. Вот и вздумали они репу сеять...	154
Медведь	Жил-был старик да старуха, детей у них не было. Старуха и говорит старику...	161A*

Fig. 2. Example of the folktale material used in the study: for every folktale text there is a corresponding motif code from ATU index

4   Approach

The problem that we are trying to solve is making a classifier of folklore texts, which, according to the text, determines the motif to which the text belongs. A zero-shot learning approach was chosen, which is explained by the specifics of the dataset: there are significantly more descriptions of motifs than texts that illustrate these motifs. In other words, it is not possible to illustrate each motif with the corresponding text. Moreover, even in the catalogs analyzed, there are plots for which there are very few or no text illustrations. In our approach, texts and descriptions of plots are presented in vector form and then transformed in such a way that the vectors of plots and descriptions that correspond to them are as close to each other as possible, i.e. so that their cosine similarity is maximal, and the cosine similarity between the text and the descriptions of plots that do not correspond to it is minimal. The data was divided into training and test sets in the proportions of 70%–30%. In case of single-label approach, the test set contains 50% of seen and 50% of unseen classes. In case of multi-label approach, the test set contains 33% of unseen classes. The model predicts on a test set, to which of 2640 motifs from the full catalog each text corresponds to.

5   Experimental Setup

5.1   Vectorizing Texts

We used Sentence RuBERT (Russian, cased, 12-layer, 768-hidden, 12-heads, 180M parameters) for vector representation of texts and motifs descriptions [6]. Motifs descriptions are short texts (109 words max), so there was no need to further process them before feeding then into the model. The texts of fairy tales are mostly long texts that exceed the maximum length limit of tokens for BERT. As a baseline approach, we cut the longer texts off and only use the first 512 tokens. We also tried the following approaches:

Extractive summarization - we used a basic TextRank summarizer from the gensim library [1]. The TextRank algorithm is a simple text summarization algorithm. It consists of the following: first, the text is divided into separate sentences. Then, for each sentence, a vector representation is formed and the similarity between the resulting vectors is considered. Then a matrix is formed in which all the measures of similarity are stored. The matrix is represented as a graph in which sentences serve as nodes and similarities as edges. Thus, the offer rank is considered. After that, the top-n most popular sentences in the text are taken [14]. In the function in gensim that was used, there is a parameter that determines what ratio of the sentences we use for the final version. In our case, this parameter is equal to 0.4: it was empirically found that this is the maximum possible parameter that allows you to represent texts in the form of no more than 512 tokens created by BERT tokenizer.

Cut into chunks and take the mean vector: the texts were divided into sentences, after which a vector was separately calculated for each sentence and the average of all sentence vectors was taken. At the moment, this approach has shown the best metrics compared to the previous two.

5.2   Models

In this study, the tasks of single-label and multi-label classification were solved - for texts with one motif and for all texts, respectively. In both cases, the approach was as follows: given a set of N texts with M corresponding motifs a N x M matrix represents the cosine similarities calculated for each possible pair of text and motif. In the case of a single label, a vector with numbers of correct text and motif matches is used as a target. In the case of a multi-label classification, the target is a matrix with labeled matches of text and motifs. Thus, the task is to maximize the cosine similarity in the correct text-motif pair and to minimize it in other cases.

Single-Label. Two approaches to single-label classification were used. In the first case, if the motif corresponded to several texts, it was repeated several times in the matrix: thus, the square matrix is being formed (Fig. 1a). This approach allows the use of symmetric cross-entropy loss: regular cross-entropy loss is calculated by row and by column of the cosine similarity matrix, after which the average of both values is taken. In the second case, if one motif corresponded to several texts, it was in the vector of motifs once, so the vector of descriptions was smaller than the vector of texts. In this approach, it is possible to use only a single cross-entropy loss. Target variables for both approaches are visualized in the image below (Fig. 3).

	Motif 1	Motif 2	Motif 1	⋮	Motif n
Text 1	1	0	0	...	0
Text 2	0	1	0	...	0
Text 3	0	0	1	...	0
...	⋮	⋮	⋮	⋱	⋮
Text n	0	0	0	...	1

(a) If a motif corresponds to many texts, it is duplicated in the matrix

	Motif 1	Motif 2	⋮	Motif n
Text 1	1	0	...	0
Text 2	0	1	...	0
Text 3	1	0	...	0
...	⋮	⋮	⋱	⋮
Text n	0	0	...	1

(b) If a motif corresponds to many texts, it occurs it matrix once

Fig. 3. Variants of the target variables used in the single-label approach. In the first case, the matrix is square, the motif is repeated several times if it corresponds to several texts. In the second case, one motif occurs once

Multi-label. In this approach, we used all the data from the dataset - texts marked up with both one and several motifs. Here, binary cross-entropy loss with logits was used, so the target was a matrix of the same dimension as the matrix of all cosine measures between motifs and texts, where the correct matches of the text and motifs were marked with ones, and the wrong matches were marked with zeros. All models were tested on the entire catalog of motifs described in the dataset chapter, which, as mentioned above, contains 2640 motif codes and their descriptions.

6 Results

Taking into account the peculiarities of the used approach to the classification of texts, it is assumed that the cosine similarity in the correct pair of folklore text and motif may not be the maximum of all of them. For example, this can be explained by the fact that the original manual markup of texts may be subjective and, as a result, not accurate enough. In this regard, it was decided to use the top k accuracy score to assess the quality of the model. The first figure shows the metrics for an approach that used a square matrix with duplicate motifs and a symmetric cross-entropy loss. The second image shows the metrics for an approach where unique motifs and a regular cross-entropy loss were used. As can be seen in the images, both approaches result in the same change in accuracy as a function of k. The third image shows the metrics for the multi-label approach. On the Y scale, in this case, it is indicated in what proportion of cases at least one of all the motifs corresponding to the text was found in the top-k predictions of the model. It is important to clarify that the training and test data are the same for all the approaches to model training and text vectorizing. The best results are shown by the approach in which the text is divided into shorter fragments and the mean vector of all texts elements is taken (Figs. 4, 5, 6 and Tables 1, 2).

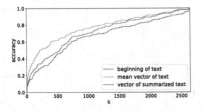

Fig. 4. Dependence of the accuracy metric on k, single-label, motifs are duplicated

Fig. 5. Dependence of the accuracy metric on k, single-label, motifs are unique

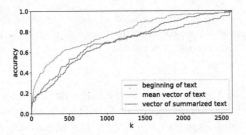

Fig. 6. Dependence of the accuracy metric on k, multi-label

Table 1. Accuracy at k = 50

	Single-label, duplicated motifs	Single-label, unique motifs	Multi-label
Beginning of text	0.15	0.22	0.14
Mean text vector	0.27	**0.37**	0.22
Summarized text	0.18	0.24	0.12

Table 2. Accuracy at k = 100

	Single-label, duplicated motifs	Single-label, unique motifs	Multi-label
Beginning of text	0.19	0.27	0.20
Mean text vector	0.35	**0.47**	0.31
Summarized text	0.25	0.31	0.19

7   Conclusion

In this work, several variants of folklore motifs classifiers according to the Aarne-Thompson index were developed. Based on the obtained metrics, it can be said that the adopted approach shows satisfactory results and the models are indeed able to predict the motifs from the text with sufficient accuracy. The metrics can also be influenced by the fact that in the data used in the research the markup can be subjective to some extent, and not all texts are marked correctly enough. As part of working with texts, we drew attention to the fact that in some cases the markup seems controversial, or there are cases when the text is marked with one motif, but it seems to contain several ones. If such text gets into the model, it can lead to incorrect representation of the text and motif vectors.

In the future, it is planned to use neural networks with a more complex architecture than those currently used, as well as to try other methods of vector text representation. Also, since one of the research problems at the moment is the small size of the dataset, it may be worth trying different ways of data augmentation [9, 17].

References

1. Barrios, F., López, F., Argerich, L., Wachenchauzer, R.: Variations of the similarity function of TextRank for automated summarization (2016)
2. Chang, M.W., Ratinov, L.A., Roth, D., Srikumar, V.: Importance of semantic representation: dataless classification. In: AAAI (2008)
3. d'Huy, J.: Folk-tale networks: a statistical approach to combinations of tale types. J. Ethnol. Folklorist. **13**(1), 29–49 (2019). https://doi.org/10.2478/jef-2019-0003
4. Gabrilovich, E., Markovitch, S.: Computing semantic relatedness using Wikipedia-based explicit semantic analysis, vol. 6 (2007)
5. Kong, L., Winestock, C., Bhatia, P.: Zero-shot medical entity retrieval without annotation: learning from rich knowledge graph semantics. CoRR abs/2105.12682 (2021). https://arxiv.org/abs/2105.12682
6. Kuratov, Y., Arkhipov, M.Y.: Adaptation of deep bidirectional multilingual transformers for Russian language. CoRR abs/1905.07213 (2019). http://arxiv.org/abs/1905.07213
7. Nakawake, Y., Sato, K.: Systematic quantitative analyses reveal the folk-zoological knowledge embedded in folktales. CoRR abs/1907.03969 (2019). http://arxiv.org/abs/1907.03969
8. Ofek, N., Daranyi, S., Rokach, L.: Linking motif sequences with tale types by machine learning. OpenAccess Ser. Inform. **32**, 166–182 (2013). https://doi.org/10.4230/OASIcs.CMN.2013.166
9. Pappas, N., Henderson, J.: Joint input-label embedding for neural text classification. CoRR abs/1806.06219 (2018). http://arxiv.org/abs/1806.06219
10. Park, B., Altieri, N., DeNero, J., Odisho, A.Y., Yu, B.: Improving natural language information extraction from cancer pathology reports using transfer learning and zero-shot string similarity. JAMIA Open **4**(3) (2021). https://doi.org/10.1093/jamiaopen/ooab085
11. Propp, V.Y.: Morfologiya skazki. Gos. in-t istorii iskusstv. L.: Academia (1928). http://feb-web.ru/feb/skazki/critics/pms/pms-001-.htm

12. Propp, V.Y.: Istoricheskie korni volshebnoj skazki. Izd-vo Leningr. gos. ordena Lenina un-ta (1946). http://feb-web.ru/feb/skazki/default.asp?/feb/skazki/critics/118-1946.html
13. Pushp, P.K., Srivastava, M.M.: Train once, test anywhere: zero-shot learning for text classification. CoRR abs/1712.05972 (2017). http://arxiv.org/abs/1712.05972
14. Rada, M., Paul, T.: TextRank: bringing order into texts (2004)
15. Radford, A., et al.: Learning transferable visual models from natural language supervision. CoRR abs/2103.00020 (2021). https://arxiv.org/abs/2103.00020
16. Song, C., Zhang, S., Sadoughi, N., Xie, P., Xing, E.P.: Generalized zero-shot ICD coding. CoRR abs/1909.13154 (2019). http://arxiv.org/abs/1909.13154
17. Yang, P., Sun, X., Li, W., Ma, S., Wu, W., Wang, H.: SGM: sequence generation model for multi-label classification. CoRR abs/1806.04822 (2018). http://arxiv.org/abs/1806.04822
18. Zhang, J., Lertvittayakumjorn, P., Guo, Y.: Integrating semantic knowledge to tackle zero-shot text classification. CoRR abs/1903.12626 (2019). http://arxiv.org/abs/1903.12626

Morphological and Emotional Features of the Speech in Children with Typical Development, Autism Spectrum Disorders and Down Syndrome

Olesia Makhnytkina[1]([✉]) [ID], Olga Frolova[2] [ID], and Elena Lyakso[2] [ID]

[1] ITMO University, Saint Petersburg 197101, Russian Federation
makhnytkina@itmo.ru

[2] Saint Petersburg State University, Saint Petersburg 199034, Russian Federation

Abstract. The paper presents the results of automatic classification of the dialogues of Russian-speaking children with typical and atypical development using machine learning methods. The study proposes an approach to developing the automatic system for classification the state of children (typical development, autism spectrum disorders, and Down syndrome) based on the linguistic characteristics of speech. 62 boys aged 8–11 years including 20 children with typical development (TD), 28 with autism spectrum disorders (ASD), and 14 with Down syndrome (DS) were interviewed. The dataset contains 69 files with dialogues between adult and child. Only children's responses were used for further analysis. Morphological, graphematic, and emotional characteristics of speech were extracted from the text of the dialogues. A total of 62 linguistic features were extracted from each dialogue: the number of replies, sentences, tokens, pauses, and unfinished words; the relative frequencies of parts of speech and some grammatical categories (animacy, number, aspect, involvement, mood, person, tense), and the statistics of positive and negative words use. The Mann-Whitney U test was used to assess differences in the linguistic features of the speech. The differences between boys with TD, ASD, and DS in 40 linguistic features of their speech were revealed. These features were used to develop classification models using machine learning methods: Gradient Boosting, Random Forest, Ada Boost. The revealed features showed a good differentiating ability. The classification accuracy for the dialogues of boys with TD, ASD and DS was 88%.

Keywords: Linguistic features · Autism spectrum disorders · Down syndrome · Automatic classification

1 Introduction

The study of speech, as a complex system, requires the use of different approaches. Traditionally, the questions of the language structure, the generation and understanding of statements, the social variability are investigated in linguistics. Depending on the studied aspects of linguistics, certain features of speech statements, for example,

V. Malykh and A. Filchenkov (Eds.): AINL 2022, CCIS 1731, pp. 49–59, 2022.
https://doi.org/10.1007/978-3-031-23372-2_5

graphematic, lexical and morphological features are analyzed. Linguistic features, for which differences have been identified for the target groups of texts, are used further for texts classification and in computational linguistics. Thus, the work [1] considers the morphological features of individual words, "adjective + noun" constructions, text dynamism, average length of words and sentences to solve the problem of classifying texts by style. Morphological and lexical features are also significant for classifying texts by gender [2] and age of authors [3]. Ontolinguistics is an independent area of linguistics [4], which studies the problems of language generation and mastering depending on the child's age, language, and social environment. Most of studies focus on the linguistics in typically developing (TD) children [4–7]. For children with atypical development, such studies are few [8, 9].

For speech annotation, specialized software can be used, further analysis is carried out manually. To study of verbs using in children with Down syndrome (DS) on the material of German language, the task of pictures description was used [10], to study subject-predicate agreement – the task of the short video (10 s) description [11]. Annotation of speech was carried out in the ELAN (EUDICO Linguistic Annotator) editor, and then the received material was analyzed manually.

The other approach is widely spread in which the annotation of the speech material is made manually by the researcher, and then an automatic analysis of the texts is performed. For revealing the differences in the use of pronouns by children with autism spectrum disorders (ASD) and TD on the material of Greek language [12], children were asked to make a story "Frog where are you" by pictures that show the story of a boy, a dog, and domestic frog [13]. Annotation of the speech materials was made independently by two experts with rechecking by a third expert, then the annotated material was translated into the CHAT (Codes for the Human Analysis of Transcripts) format for automatic analysis. In the study [14], the lexicon (frequency of use of different parts of speech), morpho-syntactic characteristics (present, past tense of verbs, plural, articles, prepositions, linking verb, etc. - 14 features in total), use of interrogative words (who, what, which, etc.) were analyzed. The average length of utterances in the spontaneous speech of children with ASD and TD was calculated using the CLAN (Computerized Language ANalysis) software [15], the annotation of the speech material was made manually.

To describe the microstructure (mean utterance length, lexical diversity, sentence structure, utterance structure, etc.) and macrostructure (story features - introduction, plot development, conclusion, etc.) of narratives of children with DS and TD [16], special software SALT (Systematic Analysis of Language Transcript, [17]) was used. In this study, children were asked to tell a story based on a series of pictures "Frog goes to dinner" [18].

The first linguistic study of high functioning ASD children's speech by automatic analysis showed the possibility of using this method for speech of children with atypical development. The use of linguistic features together with acoustic characteristics for the detection of ASD was considered in the study [19]. It was shown that the value of the F1-score in detecting children with typical development was 0.78, and for children with ASD - 0.73. In [20], the relative frequencies of using the main parts of speech were considered, the value of the F1-score for TD children was 0.93, for ASD children – 0.83, for children with DS - 0.64.

The aim of the study was to reveal the linguistic features of speech in TD children, children with ASD and DS, allowing to improve the classification of dialogues texts of these children. The study is the extension of the linguistic analysis of dialogues texts in Russian-speaking children with TD, ASD, DS [20].

2   Datasets

In our study, we used the original dataset containing hand-transcribed dialogues of children with TD, DS, and ASD. The sample included speech material of boys aged 8 to 11 years (Table 1). 62 children including 20 children with TD, 14 with DS, and 28 with ASD were interviewed. The final data set contains 69 files with dialogues. Our dataset is relatively small that is caused by difficulties in collecting of speech of children with DS and ASD [21]. The development of methods applicable to a small dataset of child speech is an important task itself [19, 22]. The choice of male children is due to the standardization of the sample by gender, linked with a higher frequency of occurrence of informants with ASD [23]. The selection of the age of informants is due to the child's sufficient verbal skills for communication with other people at this age. All children attended school (TD children attended comprehensive school, children with ASD and DS - special school). A child psychiatrist diagnosed children with ASD and DS. The CARS scale (Childhood Autism Rating Scale) [24] was used to assess the severity of autistic disorders in children with ASD. The study involved children with ASD with CARS scores of 31–42 (31–37 - moderate; 38–60 - severe form of ASD).

Table 1. Number of dialogues used in the study.

	8 y	9 y	10 y	11 y	Total
TD	5	5	5	5	20
ASD	8	10	5	12	35
DS	4	2	4	4	14

The children's speech was recorded in the school, laboratory and childcare center during the model situation - a dialogue with the experimenter. The dialogue (interview) included a standard set of questions about family, friends, walks, favorite activities, and school. The adult alternated general and specific questions in order to give the impression of a natural interaction. The experimenter's strategy was based on the maximum attraction of the child's attention; the adult's speech and behavior were emotional, but regulated by the design of the experiment.

The Marantz PMD660 digital tape recorder with a SENNHEIZER e835S extension microphone was used for audio recording. The distance from the child's face to the microphone did not exceed 50 cm (30–50 cm). The speech files were saved in the Windows PCM WAV format, 44 100 Hz, 16 bits; video files - in AVI format. At the same time, the child's behavior was video recorded using a SONY HDR-CX560E video camera.

The transcription of the dialogues was carried out by 4 experts - specialists in the field of child speech analysis. Only the replies of children were analyzed, the replies of the interviewer were deleted.

3   Methods

3.1   Graphematic Analysis of the Texts

Graphematic analysis is the primary step in the automatic natural language processing. The main task of graphematic analysis is to isolate structural units from the input text – sentences, paragraphs, words (tokens), punctuation marks, etc. Transcription of children's dialogues was made manually, which made it possible to highlight pauses in speech using punctuation marks (…). The segmentation of the text into sentences was carried out according to standard rules, if the sequence of words ends with such punctuation marks as a point, an interrogation mark, and an exclamation mark. According to the marking, the rule was used: if the sequence of words ends with a pause (…) and then the text begins with an uppercase letter, then segmentation into sentences is made; if the sequence of words ends with a pause (…) and then the text begins with a lowercase letter, then there is no division into sentences.

The example:

1: *Nu, nravyatsya … No matematika luchshe nravitsya/Well, like… But math is better. – 2 sentences.*
2: *Mne nravitsya, kak tam pechka eto … pirozhki ispekla nu … eto … eto … rebenok poteryalsya. Poshli potom ego iskat'. I vse/I like the way the stove… baked pies, well… this… this… the child is lost. Then they went to look for him. And that's all. - 3 sentences.*

The number of pauses was calculated based on the number of the sequences of symbols "…" in the text, considering pauses after unfinished words.

The example:

1: *Bol'sh… Bol'shie takie kak by, krasivye/Big… Big ones, as it were, beautiful. – 1 pause.*
2: *Bobry, belka i kak etot … Kak eto … Nu u nego meshok na gorle/Beavers, squirrel and like this… Like this… Well, he has a bag on his throat… - 3 pauses.*

The number of unfinished words was calculated based on the sequence of letters that are not the word and the presence of a pause after it (…).

The example:

1: *Bol'sh… Bol'shie takie kak by, krasivye/Big… Big ones, as it were, beautiful. - 1 unfinished word.*

2: *Bobry, belka i kak etot ... Kak eto ... Nu u nego meshok na gorle/Beavers, squirrel and like that... Like this... Well, he has a bag on his throat... - 0 unfinished words.*

After graphematic analysis, descriptive characteristics were calculated for the following features:

1. The number of replies of the respondent in the dialogue.
2. The number of sentences in the replies of the respondent in the dialogue.
3. The number of pauses in all replies of the respondent in the dialogue.
4. The average number of pauses in the reply of the respondent in the dialogue.
5. The number of unfinished words in all respondent's replies in the dialogue.
6. The average number of unfinished words in the respondent's reply in the dialogue.
7. The average number of tokens in the respondent's sentence in the dialogue.
8. The average number of tokens in the reply of the respondent in the dialogue.

3.2 Morphological Text Analysis

Morphological analysis of texts using the pymorphy2 library can be made in two modes: 1) by simple search in the OpenCorpora dictionary (http://opencorpora.org/); 2) by simple search using dictionary and rule-based predictor for unfamiliar words. For transcriptions of the dialogues of children with TD, the predictor allows to carry out a complete morphological analysis of a larger number of words, since some of the words present in our everyday speech were not in the dictionary.

The example

1. *Scooby-doo (the name of cartoon character) - noun, animate, singular;*
2. *univer (unfinished word/university/) - noun, inanimate, singular.*

However, ambiguous results were obtained for transcriptions of the dialogues of children with atypical development using a predictor:

1 *totochki (non-existent word) - noun, inanimate, singular;*
2 *luiai (non-existent word) - verb, imperfective, the speaker is not included in the action, imperative, singular;*
3 *kupatikeda (non-existent word)- noun, animate, singular;*
4 *katzeski (non-existent word) – adverb.*

Thus, further in the study, morphological analysis was carried out only on the basis of the dictionary. The creators of the dataset matched non-existent words with the words from the dictionary, and a statistical analysis of parts of speech using was made based on the morphological analysis of the word from the dictionary:

1. *schas = sejchas/now - adverb*
2. *zdras'te = zdravstvujte/hello - verb, plural, imperfective aspect, the speaker is not included in the action*

54   O. Makhnytkina et al.

After morphological analysis, the relative frequencies of the following parts of speech for each child were calculated: adjective (full) - ADJF; adjective (short) - ADJS; adverb - ADVB; comparative - COMP; conjunction - CONJ; verb (infinitive) - INFN; interjection - INTJ; non-existent word - None; noun - NOUN; pronoun-noun- NPRO; numeral - NUMR; particle - PRCL; predicative - PRED; preposition - PREP; participle (short) - PRTS; verb (personal form) - VERB.

For the most common parts of speech (noun, verb), grammemes were also defined according to the following categories from OpenCorpora (http://opencorpora.org/dict.php?act=gram):

1. category of animacy: anim - animated; inan - inanimate;
2. number: sing - singular; plur - plural;
3. category of aspect: perf - perfect aspect; impf - imperfect aspect;
4. category of involvement: incl - the speaker is included (let's go, let's go); excl - the speaker is not included in the action (go, go);
5. mood category: Indc - indicative mood; Impr - imperative mood;
6. category of person (for verbs of the future and present tense): 1per - 1 person; 2per - 2nd person; 3per - 3rd person;
7. category of tense (except for the imperative mood): pres - present tense; past - past tense; futr - future tense.

The assessment of the use of positive and negative words was carried out using the sentiment dictionary LinisCrowd 2015 (http://linis-crowd.org/). For each dialogue, a list of sentiment words was compiled and statistical measures (minimum, maximum, mean, sum, number of positive and negative score of words) were calculated.

The Mann-Whitney U test was used to test hypotheses about the difference between two independent samples in the level of the feature's expression. The choice of the Mann-Whitney U test is caused by importance of revealing differences in linguistic features between groups of children in pairs. This test is non-parametric and allows identifying the differences in the characteristics between small samples. At the second stage, datasets was formed with features that differed at the significance levels of 0.05.

To confirm the hypothesis about the significance of differences in the values of linguistic features, the problem of classifying dialogues was solved based on the classical machine learning methods, considering the psychoneurological state of children. As a basic method, Gradient Boosted Decision Trees was used, which showed good results in solving the problem of classifying texts in children with TD and ASD [19]. Gradient boosting is an ensemble of decision trees that are trained sequentially. In order to improve the quality of classification, other ensembles of models based on decision trees are considered: Random Forest, AdaBoost. Since the data set used in the study is small, the standard division of data into training and test sets can lead to large differences in the accuracy of prediction by model, depending on which data are included in the test and training sets. Thereby the LeaveOneOut cross-validation method was used to evaluate the generalizing ability of the considered classification algorithms. All methods discussed were implemented using the scikit-learn library in Python[1].

---
[1] https://scikit-learn.org/stable/

4 Results

The study [20] showed differences at a significance level of 0.001 observed for the features: "relative frequency of adjectives (full)", "relative frequency of adverbs", "relative frequency of comparatives", "relative frequency of conjunctions", "relative frequency of verbs (infinitive)", "relative frequency of non-existent words", "relative frequency of noun-pronouns", "relative frequency of prepositions". Table 2 presents the results for the new text features.

Table 2. Differences in the speech of children with typical and atypical development.

Cathegory		TD	DS	ASD
NOUN_plur	TD		+***	+***
	DS	+***		−
	ASD	+***	−	
NOUN_sing	TD		+**	+***
	DS	+**		−
	ASD	+***	−	
NOUN_anim	TD		−	+**
	DS	−		−
	ASD	+**	−	
NOUN_anim	TD		−	+**
	DS	−		−
	ASD	+**	−	
NOUN_inan	TD		+*	+**
	DS	+*		−
	ASD	+**	−	
VERB_plur	TD		+***	+**
	DS	+***		−
	ASD	+**	−	
VERB_impf	TD		+***	+*
	DS	+***		−
	ASD	+*	−	
VERB_excl	TD		−	−
	DS	−		+*
	ASD	−	+*	
VERB_None	TD		+***	+*

(*continued*)

Table 2. (*continued*)

Cathegory		TD	DS	ASD
	DS	+***		+**
	ASD	+*	+**	
VERB_impr	TD		−	−
	DS	−		+*
	ASD	−	+*	
VERB_indc	TD		+***	+*
	DS	+***		+**
	ASD	+*	+**	
VERB_past	TD		+***	+**
	DS	+***		+*
	ASD	+**	+*	
VERB_pres	TD		+*	+*
	DS	+*		−
	ASD	+*	−	
VERB_1per	TD		+***	+***
	DS	+***		−
	ASD	+***	−	
The maximum score of sentiment words	TD		+**	+*
	DS	+**		
	ASD	+*		
Number of positive words' score	TD		+*	+*
	DS	+*		
	ASD	+*		

"−" – no differences, "+" – significant differences, "*" – significant differences at the level p < 0.05, "**" –significant differences at the level p < 0.01, "***" –significant differences at the level p < 0.001.

The analysis showed significant differences in the speech of children with DS and TD, children with ASD and TD. Significant differences in the verbs use (the category of number, aspect, mood, tense, person), nouns (the category of number, the category of animacy) and in the specificity of the verbal manifestation of emotions - the use of positive words are observed. Differences between children with DS and ASD were found only in the verb use (category of involvement, mood, tense) (Table 3).

Using the RandomForestClassifier to predict class labels achieved an accuracy of 88%. As a result, 95% of the dialogues of children with TD were correctly classified (19 from 20, one dialogue was attributed to ASD). For children with atypical development, 71% of the dialogues of children with DS (11 from 14, 3 dialogues were attributed

Table 3. Classification results.

Method	Diagnose	Precision	Recall	F1- score	Accuracy
GradientBoostingClassifier	TD	0.89	0.80	0.84	0.75
	DS	0.60	0.64	0.62	
	ASD	0.75	0.77	0.76	
RandomForestClassifier	**TD**	**0.90**	**0.95**	**0.93**	**0.88**
	DS	**0.91**	**0.71**	**0.80**	
	ASD	**0.86**	**0.91**	**0.89**	
AdaBoostClassifier	TD	0.90	0.95	0.93	0.83
	DS	0.67	0.71	0.69	
	ASD	0.85	0.80	0.82	
Makhnytkina, 2021 [20]	TD	0.90	0.95	0.93	0.83
	DS	0.73	0.57	0.64	
	ASD	0.81	0.86	0.83	
Cho, 2019 [19]	TD	0.71	0.86	0.78	0.76
	ASD	0.82	0.66	0.73	

to ASD), 91% of the dialogues of children with ASD (31 from 35, 2 dialogues were attributed to the dialogue of children with TD and 2 to the dialogues of children with DS) were correctly classified. The results of the experiments significantly exceed the baseline [19]. However, this may be due, among other things, to the different severity of ASD in children in our experiment and the experiments of the colleagues. The resulting solution also exceeds the results obtained in [20] due to the consideration of new morphological features and the sentiment of words.

5   Conclusions and Discussion

The paper presents the results of automatic classification of the dialogues of boys with TD, DS, ASD using machine learning methods. To develop a set of features that allow classification at a sufficiently high level, linguistic features of the dialogues of children with typical and atypical development were identified. A total of 62 features were considered, and only 40 of them are distinctive for the groups. The approach based on the use of the RandomForestClassifier made it possible to achieve an accuracy of 88% of dialogue classification, the best quality was achieved for the dialogues of children with TD (recall = 95%) and children with ASD (recall = 91%), and the worst - for children with DS (recall = 71%). On average, the values of significant linguistic features of the dialogues in children with ASD are between the values of the features of the dialogues of TD and DS children.

Perceptual studies showed that listeners had recognize better the emotional state of children with ASD and DS than the state of TD peers on the base of their speech [25, 26].

Number of studies, for example [19], show that for improving the classifying accuracy of the dialogues in children with typical and atypical development, it is useful to combine audio and text modalities. Considering our experience in automatic classification of TD children's emotional states [27, 28] and diagnoses of children with atypical development [22] by sounding speech, in the future we plan to combine the results of classifying children's diagnoses by audio and text modality based on the features proposed in this article, which can improve the quality of classification models.

The results of our study are useful for developing the automatic systems of early diagnostics of developmental disorders and could be used by different specialists working with children.

Acknowledgment. The research was financially supported by Russian Science Foundation (project 22-45-02007).

References

1. Dubovik, A.R.: Automatic determination of the stylistic affiliation of texts by their statistical parameters. Computational Linguistics and Computational Ontologies **1**, 29–45 (on Russian) (2017)
2. Sboev, A., Litvinova, T., Gudovskikh, D., Rybka, R., Moloshnikov, I.: Machine learning models of text categorization by author gender using topic-independent features. Procedia Comput. Sci. **101**, 135–142 (2016). https://doi.org/10.1016/j.procs.2016.11.017
3. Cheng, J.K., Fernandez, A., Quindoza, R.G.M., Tan, S., Cheng, C.: A Model for age and gender profiling of social media accounts based on post contents. In: Cheng, L., Leung, A.C.S., Ozawa, S. (eds.) ICONIP 2018. LNCS, vol. 11302, pp. 113–123. Springer, Cham (2018). https://doi.org/10.1007/978-3-030-04179-3_10
4. Tseitlin, S.N.: Language and Child: Linguistics of Children's Speech: Textbook. VLADOS, Moscow (on Russian) (2000)
5. Eliseeva, M.B.: The formation of the individual language system of the child. Early stages. Publisher, Languages of Slavic Culture, Moscow (on Russian) (2015)
6. Feldman, H.M.: How young children learn language and speech. Pediatr. Rev. **40**(8), 398–411 (2019). https://doi.org/10.1542/pir.2017-0325
7. McCreery, R.W., Miller, M.K., Buss, E., Leibold, L.J.: Cognitive and linguistic contributions to masked speech recognition in children. J. Speech Lang. Hear. Res. **63**(10), 3525–3538 (2020). https://doi.org/10.1044/2020_JSLHR-20-00030
8. Lyakso, E.E., Frolova, O.V.: Analysis of speech texts "adult-child", "adult-adult" with typical and atypical development of informants. Theoretical and Applied Linguistics **2**, 20–47 (on Russian) (2017)
9. Nikolaev, A.S., Frolova, O.V., Gorodnyj, V.A., Lyakso, E.E.: Characteristics of response replies of 5–11 years old children with autism spectrum disorders in dialogues with adults. Questions of Psycholinguistics **4**(42), 92–105 (on Russian) (2019)
10. Penke, M.: Regular and irregular inflection in down syndrome - New evidence from German. Cortex **116**, 192–208 (2019). https://doi.org/10.1016/j.cortex.2018.08.010
11. Penke, M.: Verbal agreement inflection in German children with down syndrome. J. Speech Lang. Hear. Res. **61**(9), 2217–2234 (2018). https://doi.org/10.1044/2018_JSLHR-L-17-0241
12. Terzi, A., Marinis, T., Zafeiri, A., Francis, K.: Subject and object pronouns in high-functioning children with ASD of a null-subject language. Front. Psychol. **10**, 1301 (2019). https://doi.org/10.3389/fpsyg.2019.01301

13. Mayer, M.: Frog, where are you? Dial Press, New York (1969)
14. Tek, S., Mesite, L., Fein, D., Naigles, L.: Longitudinal analyses of expressive language development reveal two distinct language profiles among young children with autism spectrum disorders. J. Autism Dev. Disord. **44**(1), 75–89 (2013). https://doi.org/10.1007/s10803-013-1853-4
15. MacWhinney, B.: The CHILDES Project: Tools for Analyzing Talk. Lawrence Erlbaum Associates, NY (1995)
16. Hessling, A., Brimo, D.M.: Spoken fictional narrative and literacy skills of children with Down syndrome. J. Commun. Disord. **79**, 76–89 (2019). https://doi.org/10.1016/j.jcomdis.2019.03.005
17. Miller, J., Chapman, R.S.: Systematic Analysis of Language Transcripts (SALT). Language Analysis Laboratory, Waisman Center, Madison, WI (1990)
18. Mayer, M.: Frog Goes to Dinner. Dial Press, New York (1969)
19. Cho, S., Liberman, M., Ryant, N., Cola, M., Schultz, R.T., Parish-Morris, J.: Automatic detection of Autism Spectrum Disorder in children using acoustic and text features from brief natural conversations. In: Interspeech 2019: 20th Annual Conference of the International Speech Communication Association, pp. 2513–2517. Graz, Austria (2019). https://doi.org/10.21437/Interspeech.2019-1452
20. Makhnytkina, O., Grigorev, A., Nikolaev, A.: Analysis of dialogues of typically developing children, children with down syndrome and ASD using machine learning methods. In: Karpov, A., Potapova, R. (eds.) SPECOM 2021. LNCS (LNAI), vol. 12997, pp. 397–406. Springer, Cham (2021). https://doi.org/10.1007/978-3-030-87802-3_36
21. Lyakso E.E., Frolova O.V. Recording the speech of children with atypical development: peculiarities and perspectives. In: ICMI 2021 Companion - Companion Publication of the 2021 International Conference on Multimodal Interaction, pp. 408–413. Montreal, Canada (2021). https://doi.org/10.1145/3461615.3485439
22. Matveev, Y., Matveev, A., Frolova, O., Lyakso, E.: Automatic recognition of the psychoneurological state of children: autism spectrum disorders, down syndrome, typical development. In: Karpov, A., Potapova, R. (eds.) SPECOM 2021. LNCS (LNAI), vol. 12997, pp. 417–425. Springer, Cham (2021). https://doi.org/10.1007/978-3-030-87802-3_38
23. Nicholas, J.S., Charles, J.M., Carpenter, L.A., King, L.B., Jenner, W., Spratt, E.G.: Prevalence and characteristics of children with autism-spectrum disorders. Ann. Epidemiol. **18**(2), 130–136 (2008). https://doi.org/10.1016/j.annepidem.2007.10.013
24. Schopler, E., Reichler, R.J., DeVellis, R.F., Daly, K.: Toward objective classification of childhood autism: Childhood Autism Rating Scale (CARS). J. Autism Dev. Disord. **10**(1), 91–103 (1980). https://doi.org/10.1007/BF02408436
25. Lyakso, E.E., Frolova, O.V., Grigor'ev, A.S., Sokolova, V.D., Yarotskaya, K.A.: Recognition by adults of emotional state in typically developing children and children with autism spectrum disorders. Neurosci. Behav. Physiol. **47**(9), 1051–1059 (2017). https://doi.org/10.1007/s11055-017-0511-2
26. Lyakso, E., Frolova, O., Gorodnyi, V., Grigorev, A., Nikolaev, A., Matveev, Y.: Reflection of the emotional state in the characteristics of voice and speech of children with Down syndrome. In: Proceedings of 10th International Conference on Speech Technology and Human-Computer Dialogue, SpeD, 8906579. IEEE, Timisoara, Romania (2019). https://doi.org/10.1109/SPED.2019.8906579
27. Lyakso, E., et al.: EmoChildRu: emotional child russian speech corpus. In: Ronzhin, A., Potapova, R., Fakotakis, N. (eds.) SPECOM 2015. LNCS (LNAI), vol. 9319, pp. 144–152. Springer, Cham (2015). https://doi.org/10.1007/978-3-319-23132-7_18
28. Kaya, H., Salah, A.A., Karpov, A., Frolova, O., Grigorev, A., Lyakso, E.: Emotion, age, and gender classification in children's speech by humans and machines. Comput. Speech Lang. **46**, 268–283 (2017). https://doi.org/10.1016/j.csl.2017.06.002

WikiMulti: A Corpus for Cross-Lingual Summarization

Pavel Tikhonov[1]([✉]) and Valentin Malykh[2]

[1] National Research University Higher School of Economics, Moscow, Russia
pav3370@yandex.ru
[2] Kazan Federal University, Kazan, Russia
valentin.malykh@phystech.edu

Abstract. Cross-lingual summarization (CLS) is the task to produce a summary in one particular language for a source document in a different language. We introduce WikiMulti - a new dataset for cross-lingual summarization based on Wikipedia articles in 15 languages. As a set of baselines for further studies, we evaluate the performance of existing cross-lingual abstractive summarization methods on our dataset. We make our dataset publicly available here: https://github.com/tikhonovpavel/wikimulti.

1 Introduction

Automatic summarization is one of the central problems in Natural Language Processing (NLP) posing several challenges relating to understanding (i.e. identifying important content) and generation (i.e. aggregating and rewording the identified content into a summary). Of the many summarization paradigms that have been identified over the years, single-document summarization has consistently garnered attention. Given an input text (typically a long document or article), the goal is to generate a smaller, concise piece of text that conveys the key information of the input text. There are two main approaches to automatic text summarization: extractive and abstractive. Extractive methods chop out one or more segments from the input text and concatenate them to produce a summary. These methods were dominant in the early era of summarization, but they suffer from some limitations, including weak coherence between sentences, inability to simplify complex and long sentences, and unintended repetition. Abstractive text summarization is the task of generating a short and concise summary that captures the salient ideas of the source text.

Despite the presence of a large number of datasets for abstractive summarization [11,12,14], the vast majority of them are focused on *mono-lingual* summarization.

However, there exists a number of summarization datasets including several languages. The task for summarization on several languages could be stated in two significantly different ways. The one is called *cross-lingual* and other is *multi-lingual*. In the case of multilingual datasets, the corpus is collected in several languages, but there is no requirement for an alignment, in the sense that the documents in one language may not correspond to the documents in any other language. The systems trained on such corpora are targeted to produce summary of a document of the same language, e.g. a system should make summaries for Portuguese documents in form of the paragraphs in Portuguese. *Multiling'13 and '15* [2,4,5], MLSUM [15], and XL-Sum [6] are examples of multilingual datasets.

In the case of a cross-lingual dataset, the corpus have to be aligned between the languages. For example, the document in English should have a summary in Portuguese. The systems trained on such datasets should be able to make a summary in another language regarding the language of the input document.

There were a few attempts for addressing the problem of cross-lingual summarization [7,13]. Among them, only [7] is the only one of the datasets which is large and addresses the problem of cross-lingual summarization. However, this dataset contains only short articles for a few topics.

This further opens up avenues to explore new approaches for cross-lingual summarization, which are currently understudied. We present a novel dataset **WikiMulti** consisting of Wikipedia articles and summaries in 15 languages. With the dataset in hand, we evaluate several approaches for cross-lingual summarization to establish the baselines.

This paper is structured as follows: in Sect. 2 we review existing datasets on multi- and cross-lingual summarization; in Sect. 3 we describe WikiMulti, the presented dataset; Sect. 4 is devoted to the description of the baselines for this dataset; Sect. 5 contains the results for the baselines, while Sect. 6 concludes the paper.

2   Existing Datasets

In this section, we take a closer look at the multi- and cross-lingual summarization datasets. The statistics on these datasets provided in Table 1.

Table 1. Statistics for existing multi-lingual (top) and cross-lingual (bottom) datasets. Lengths specified in number of words.

	Num languages	Avg num summaries	Avg summary length	Avg article length
MULTILING'15	40	30	185	4,111
XL-SUM	44	22,847	153	3,024
MLSUM	5	314,208	34	812
GLOBAL VOICES	15	1,456	51	359
WIKILINGUA	18	42,783	39	391
WIKIMULTI	15	10,467	112	1078

2.1   Multi-lingual Datasets

Multiling'13 [2,4] and **Multiling'15** [5] have been collected at MultiLing Workshops by organizers. The MultiLing13 dataset includes summaries of 30 Wikipedia articles per language, describing a given topic. For MultiLing'15, an additional 30 documents were collected for evaluation purposes.

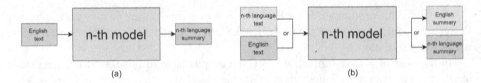

Fig. 1. (a) - one-directional approach. (b) - two-directional approach

MLSUM [15]: A dataset obtained from online newspapers. It contains 1.5 million article/summary pairs in five different languages, namely, French, German, Spanish, Russian, and Turkish.

XL-Sum [6]: A dataset containing 1 million article-summary pairs in 44 languages, being the first publicly available abstractive summarization dataset for many of them. The dataset covers 44 languages ranging from low to high-resource.

2.2 Cross-Lingual Datasets

Global Voices [13]: authors collected descriptions of news articles provided by Global Voices site creators (it's an international, multilingual community of writers, translators, academics, and digital rights activists.). This dataset supports 15 languages, however, 10 of them have less than 1,000 articles.

WikiLingua [7]: authors crawled WikiHow site (is an online resource of how-to guides where each page includes multiple methods for completing a multi-step procedural task along with a one-sentence summary of each step).

3 WikiMulti Dataset

The well-known community collected encyclopedic resource of Wikipedia is a source for many datasets [1, 16, 17] to name a few, due to on the one hand the massive contents with a variety of topics and languages, curation of the content (for the most popular languages), and on the other hand, the permissive Creative Common license[1] used throughout the whole Wikipedia.

Wikipedia project has a concept of so-called Good Article, i.e. the article which is approved by the community as the one describing a specific topic in full detail and well written. One point of this article structure includes the summary as the first paragraph of an article. We decided to build our dataset on this basis. To produce the corpus, we take a list of Wikipedia's Good Articles[2] and get a corresponding article in 14 other languages for each article in the list.

---

[1] "Text is available under the Creative Commons Attribution-ShareAlike License 3.0", https://en.wikipedia.org/wiki/Main_Page.

[2] https://en.wikipedia.org/wiki/Wikipedia:Good_articles/all
https://en.wikipedia.org/wiki/Wikipedia:Good_articles/Social_sciences_and_society
https://en.wikipedia.org/wiki/Wikipedia:Good_articles/Sports_and_recreation
https://en.wikipedia.org/wiki/Wikipedia:Good_articles/Video_games
https://en.wikipedia.org/wiki/Wikipedia:Good_articles/Warfare.

Each article belongs to some categories and subcategories. For example category "Language and literature" is divided into "Ancient texts", "Comics", "Novels", "Characters and fictional items", etc. The dataset contains categories from "Architecture - Bridges and tunnels" to "Video game history and development", 49 categories in total. The statistics of the articles in the categories for English could be found in Table B.

A typical Wikipedia article is structured as follows: the first paragraph consisting of 3–7 sentences describes the subject of the article briefly. While the rest of the article contains the details. We use the first paragraph as a summary and the rest of the article as a text to summarize. The samples from the collected dataset can be seen in Table 2.

Our final dataset consists of 22,061 unique English articles. Other languages have, on average, 9,639 articles that align with an article in English. From the list of Wikipedias[3], those with more than 1 million articles were selected. Several of such Wikipedias were skipped (namely, Waray, Cebuano, Egyptian Arabic) because the most articles have one or two paragraphs.

More detailed statistics for our dataset is shown at Table 3 while its comparison to other existing cross-lingual datasets is shown in Table 1.

4   Experiments

In all the experiments we used classic ROUGE scores described in [8] for evaluation in our experiments. We use all the most common variances of ROUGE scores, namely, Precision, Recall, and F-measure for ROUGE-1, ROUGE-2, and ROUGE-L.

4.1   Baselines

We evaluate the following baseline approaches for cross-lingual summarization on our data:

TextRank+Translate: we have used TextRank [10] tool to automatically get a summary of the text without using complex models, and then translate summary to target language. Following the recommendation from [7] we used Amazon translating tool[4] to perform translation.

Also we fine-tuned several models to perform cross-lingual summarization task to do direct cross-lingual learning. Fine tuning on different models might give a better idea of which architectures are best suited. We've used the following models:

mBART [9] is a multi-lingual language model that has been trained on large, monolingual corpora in 25 languages. The model uses a shared sub-word vocabulary, encoder, and decoder across all 25 languages, and is trained as a denoising auto-encoder during the pre-training step. mBART is trained once for all languages, providing a set of parameters that can be fine-tuned for any of the language pairs in both supervised and unsupervised settings, without any task-specific or language-specific modifications or initialization schemes.

---

[3] https://en.wikipedia.org/wiki/List_of_Wikipedias.
[4] https://aws.amazon.com/translate/.

Table 2. Example summaries from WikiMulti for Wikipedia artile "Outer Space".

L	Summary
EN	Outer space, commonly shortened to space, is the expanse that exists beyond Earth and its atmosphere and between celestial bodies. Outer space is not completely empty-it is a hard vacuum containing a low density of particles, predominantly a plasma of hydrogen and helium, as well as electromagnetic radiation, magnetic fields, neutrinos, dust, and cosmic rays. The baseline temperature of outer space, as set by the background radiation from the Big Bang, is 2.7 kelvins ($-270.45\,°C$; $-454.81\,°F$). The plasma between galaxies is thought to account for about half of the baryonic (ordinary) matter in the universe, having a number density of less than one hydrogen atom per cubic metre and a temperature of millions of kelvins. Local concentrations of matter have condensed into stars and galaxies. Studies indicate that 90% of the mass in most galaxies is in an unknown form, called dark matter, which interacts with other matter through gravitational but not electromagnetic forces. Observations suggest that the majority of the mass-energy in the observable universe is dark energy, a type of vacuum energy that is poorly understood. Intergalactic space takes up most of the volume of the universe, but even galaxies and star systems consist almost entirely of empty space
FR	L'espace désigne les zones de l'Univers situées au-delà des atmosphères et des corps célestes. Il s'agit de l'étendue de densité quasi nulle qui sépare les astres. On parle aussi de vide spatial. Selon les endroits de l'espace désignés, on le qualifie quelquefois d'espace cislunaire, interplanétaire, interstellaire (ou intersidéral) et intergalactique pour désigner plus précisément le vide spatial qui est délimité respectivement par le système Terre-Lune, les planètes, les étoiles et les galaxies. L'espace peut aussi se dééfinir en opposition à l'atmosphère terrestre
DE	Der Weltraum bezeichnet den Raum zwischen Himmelskörpern. Die Atmosphären von festen und gasförmigen Himmelskörpern (wie Sternen und Planeten) haben keine feste Grenze nach oben, sondern werden mit zunehmendem Abstand zum Himmelskörper allmählich immer dünner. Ab einer bestimmten Höhe spricht man vom Beginn des Weltraums. Im Weltraum herrscht ein Hochvakuum mit niedriger Teilchendichte. Er ist aber kein leerer Raum, sondern enthält Gase, kosmischen Staub und Elementarteilchen (Neutrinos, kosmische Strahlung, Partikel), außerdem elektrische und magnetische Felder, Gravitationsfelder und elektromagnetische Wellen (Photonen). Das fast vollständige Vakuum im Weltraum macht ihn außerordentlich durchsichtig und erlaubt die Beobachtung extrem entfernter Objekte, etwa anderer Galaxien. Jedoch können Nebel aus interstellarer Materie die Sicht auf dahinterliegende Objekte auch stark behindern
NL	De ruimte of kosmische ruimte is in de astronomie en voor het onderscheid tussen luchtvaart en ruimtevaart het deel van het heelal op meer dan 100 km van de Aarde. Deze grens is de Kármánlijn, hoewel het geen lijn is, maar een boloppervlak. Er is nog wel discussie of een hoogte van 80 km niet meer voldoet aan relevante natuurkundige criteria. Deep space is het deel van het heelal op grotere afstand dan de Aarde-Maan-lagrangepunten, ruim verder dan de Maan. De ruimte is geen echt vacuüm, maar bestaat hoofdzakelijk uit plasma van waterstof en helium, elektromagnetische straling (in het bijzonder kosmische achtergrondstraling) en neutrino's. De ruimte bevat zeer weinig atomen van andere elementen (metalen) en stofdeeltjes. De intergalactische ruimte bevat slechts enkele waterstofatomen per kubieke centimeter (in ingeademde lucht zitten ongeveer 1019 atomen per kubieke centimeter). Volgens de meeste theorieën is de ruimte daarnaast rijk aan donkere energie en donkere materie. Ook kunnen er objecten doorheen bewegen, zoals meteoroïden en kometen

Table 3. Number of articles on different languages in WikiMulti.

Language	Language code	Articles
English	EN	22061
French	FR	14625
Spanish	ES	13068
Italian	IT	11847
Russian	RU	11703
German	DE	11228
Portuguese	PT	10441
Japanese	JA	8922
Polish	PL	8875
Chinese	ZH	8711
Swedish	SV	8007
Dutch	NL	7681
Arabic	AR	7476
Ukranian	UK	7216
Vietnamese	VI	5153
Average		9639

M2M100 [3] is a multilingual encoder-decoder (seq-to-seq) model primarily intended for translation task. It was originally pre-trained on a dataset that covers thousands of language directions with supervised data, created through large-scale mining. One of the main goals stated by the authors is to focus on a non-English-centric approach: the model can translate directly between any pair of 100 languages.

mT5 [18] is a massive model, a multilingual variant of T5 that was pre-trained on a Common Crawl-based dataset covering 101 languages. The model was trained with "Text-to-Text Transfer Transformer" paradigm which means casting every task, including translation, question answering and classification as feeding the model text as input and training it to generate some target text. This allows to use the same model, loss function, hyperparameters, etc. across diverse set of tasks.

To train M2M100 and mBART we took a one-directional approach: train 14 different models using English as source language and summarize English text into one of 14 languages. I.e. for a French-English pair, all texts will be in English and the model will summarize them into French.

To train mT5 we took a different two-directional approach: train 14 different models, but use both English and non-English articles as text to summarize and as summaries 50% of time. In this case for the same French-English pair, half of the texts will be in English, and the model will summarize them in French, and the other half of the texts will be in French, and the model will summarize them into English.

Figure 1 illustrates these two kinds of approaches.

4.2   Experimental Setup

We fine-tuned mT5, M2M100 and mBART models for 20k steps on a distributed cluster of 7 Nvidia Tesla P100 GPUs. We used AdamW with cosine learning rate schedule with a linear warmup of 500 steps.

5   Results and Analysis

Table A shows ROUGE scores for the evaluated baselines. M2M100 showed the highest performance on average, especially compared to mBART and mT5. However, all three M2M100, TextRank+Translate, and mBART have problems with Japanese and Chinese languages, where mT5 is better than all the others. Also, it is interesting that for the Dutch language, all models show on average a larger ROUGE score than in other languages.

6   Conclusion

We proposed a novel dataset for cross-lingual summarization. It is comparable in size to the existing largest one, while being more broad in topics and including longer documents and summaries. We have evaluated several well known models for summarization on this dataset and found out that the performance is strongly correlated with the language itself than the model. E.g. the Dutch language has better scores on average for all the models. We hypothesize that this reflects the culture of Wikipedia writing in Dutch language, rather than the language structure.

We hope that this dataset will ease the way for other researchers in the field of cross-lingual summarization.

Acknowledgements. The work of the last author was funded by RFBR, project number 19-37-60027.

Appendix

A   Evaluation results for the baseline models on WikiMulti

Model	Language	ROUGE-1			ROUGE-2			ROUGE-L		
		F	P	R	F	P	R	F	P	R
TEXTRANK+TRANSLATE	AR	0.11	0.10	0.15	0.02	0.01	0.02	0.10	0.08	0.12
	DE	0.14	0.11	0.23	0.02	0.01	0.04	0.12	0.09	0.20
	ES	0.21	0.17	0.28	0.04	0.03	0.06	0.17	0.14	0.24
	FR	0.20	0.16	0.31	0.04	0.03	0.08	0.17	0.13	0.27
	IT	0.18	0.15	0.27	0.03	0.02	0.05	0.16	0.13	0.23
	JA	0.01	0.01	0.01	0.00	0.00	0.00	0.01	0.01	0.01
	NL	0.18	0.14	0.31	0.04	0.03	0.07	0.16	0.12	0.28
	PL	0.10	0.07	0.19	0.02	0.01	0.04	0.09	0.07	0.17
	PT	0.18	0.15	0.25	0.02	0.02	0.04	0.15	0.13	0.22
	RU	0.08	0.06	0.14	0.01	0.01	0.02	0.07	0.06	0.13
	SV	0.15	0.11	0.26	0.02	0.01	0.04	0.14	0.10	0.23
	UK	0.07	0.05	0.12	0.01	0.01	0.02	0.06	0.05	0.11
	VI	0.21	0.18	0.30	0.04	0.03	0.06	0.18	0.15	0.26
	ZH	0.00	0.00	0.00	0.00	0.00	0.00	0.00	0.00	0.00
M2M100	AR	0.20	0.31	0.16	0.08	0.11	0.07	0.19	0.29	0.15
	DE	0.29	0.42	0.24	0.13	0.17	0.11	0.27	0.39	0.23
	ES	0.34	0.46	0.30	0.17	0.22	0.16	0.32	0.43	0.28
	FR	0.28	0.49	0.22	0.13	0.22	0.10	0.26	0.45	0.21
	IT	0.25	0.44	0.19	0.09	0.17	0.07	0.23	0.41	0.18
	JA	0.08	0.10	0.07	0.03	0.03	0.03	0.08	0.10	0.07
	NL	0.38	0.48	0.34	0.20	0.24	0.19	0.36	0.46	0.33
	PL	0.31	0.37	0.29	0.17	0.19	0.16	0.30	0.36	0.29
	PT	0.31	0.43	0.26	0.14	0.19	0.13	0.28	0.39	0.24
	SV	0.31	0.40	0.28	0.14	0.18	0.14	0.30	0.38	0.27
	UK	0.27	0.36	0.25	0.14	0.17	0.14	0.27	0.35	0.25
	VI	0.33	0.42	0.30	0.16	0.20	0.15	0.31	0.38	0.28
	ZH	0.03	0.04	0.03	0.01	0.01	0.01	0.03	0.04	0.03
MBART	AR	0.15	0.17	0.14	0.10	0.12	0.08	0.16	0.12	0.14
	DE	0.19	0.23	0.18	0.05	0.06	0.05	0.18	0.22	0.17
	ES	0.32	0.44	0.29	0.16	0.20	0.15	0.30	0.41	0.27
	FR	0.30	0.50	0.24	0.14	0.24	0.12	0.29	0.47	0.23
	IT	0.16	0.22	0.14	0.02	0.03	0.02	0.14	0.19	0.13
	JA	0.04	0.05	0.03	0.00	0.00	0.00	0.04	0.05	0.03
	NL	0.41	0.47	0.39	0.23	0.26	0.23	0.39	0.45	0.37
	PL	0.21	0.23	0.21	0.09	0.09	0.08	0.20	0.22	0.21
	PT	0.19	0.23	0.18	0.06	0.07	0.06	0.17	0.22	0.16
	RU	0.26	0.32	0.24	0.11	0.14	0.11	0.26	0.32	0.23
	SV	0.30	0.37	0.27	0.13	0.15	0.12	0.29	0.35	0.26
	UK	0.21	0.27	0.20	0.08	0.11	0.08	0.21	0.26	0.19
	VI	0.16	0.17	0.17	0.03	0.03	0.03	0.14	0.15	0.15
	ZH	0.01	0.00	0.01	0.00	0.00	0.00	0.01	0.03	0.02
MT5	AR	0.17	0.37	0.12	0.05	0.10	0.04	0.16	0.35	0.11
	DE	0.30	0.44	0.25	0.13	0.17	0.12	0.29	0.42	0.25
	ES	0.29	0.49	0.23	0.13	0.21	0.10	0.28	0.47	0.22
	FR	0.28	0.47	0.22	0.11	0.19	0.09	0.26	0.44	0.20
	IT	0.29	0.49	0.23	0.14	0.22	0.11	0.28	0.46	0.22
	JA	0.16	0.25	0.13	0.06	0.08	0.05	0.16	0.25	0.12
	NL	0.32	0.49	0.26	0.13	0.20	0.11	0.30	0.47	0.25
	PL	0.23	0.39	0.18	0.08	0.13	0.07	0.22	0.38	0.18
	PT	0.29	0.42	0.25	0.13	0.17	0.12	0.28	0.40	0.24
	SV	0.28	0.43	0.23	0.12	0.18	0.10	0.27	0.42	0.22
	UK	0.22	0.38	0.18	0.08	0.13	0.07	0.22	0.37	0.17
	VI	0.27	0.43	0.23	0.11	0.17	0.10	0.26	0.40	0.21
	ZH	0.13	0.22	0.10	0.04	0.06	0.03	0.13	0.21	0.10

B   English Good articles divided into categories

Category	Num of articles	Num of subcategories
Agriculture, food, and drink	298	10
Albums	1350	13
Architecture	1062	11
Art	368	3
Biology and medicine	1889	21
Chemistry and materials science	184	14
Classical compositions	137	2
Computing and engineering	383	11
Earth science	1357	15
Film	1157	18
Geography	666	9
Language and literature	1308	17
Mathematics and mathematicians	110	3
Media and drama	657	6
Other music articles	878	7
Philosophy	216	6
Physics and astronomy	398	11
Places	533	10
Religion	424	5
Royalty, nobility, and heraldry	684	4
Songs	2246	23
Television	2586	113
Transport	2404	17
World history	1629	14
Armies and military units	384	4
Baseball	431	2
Basketball	251	2
Battles, exercises, and conflicts	1051	10
Cricket	139	2
Culture, sociology, and psychology	381	8
Economics and business	317	5
Education	280	3
Football	1394	7
Hockey	264	3
Law	543	10
Magazines and print journalism	151	2
Military aircraft	151	2
Military decorations and memorials	24	2
Military people	797	7
Military ranks and positions	7	1
Motorsport	317	2
Multi-sport event	421	5
Other sports	841	31
Politics and government	654	11
Pro wrestling	344	5
Recreation	278	9
Video games	1639	20
Warships and naval units	1761	3
Weapons, equipment, and buildings	336	4

References

1. Chen, D., Fisch, A., Weston, J., Bordes, A.: Reading wikipedia to answer open-domain questions. arXiv preprint. arXiv:1704.00051 (2017)
2. Elhadad, M., Miranda-Jiménez, S., Steinberger, J., Giannakopoulos, G.: Multi-document multilingual summarization corpus preparation, part 2: Czech, hebrew and spanish. In: Proceedings of the MultiLing 2013 Workshop on Multilingual Multi-document Summarization, pp. 13–19 (2013)
3. Fan, A., et al.: Beyond English-centric multilingual machine translation. J. Mach. Learn. Res. **22**(107), 1–48 (2021)
4. Giannakopoulos, G.: Multi-document multilingual summarization and evaluation tracks in acl 2013 multiling workshop. In: Proceedings of the Multiling 2013 Workshop on Multilingual Multi-document Summarization, pp. 20–28 (2013)
5. Giannakopoulos, G., et al.: Multiling 2015: multilingual summarization of single and multi-documents, on-line fora, and call-center conversations. In: Proceedings of the 16th Annual Meeting of the Special Interest Group on Discourse and Dialogue, pp. 270–274 (2015)
6. Hasan, T.: Xl-sum: large-scale multilingual abstractive summarization for 44 languages. arXiv preprint. arXiv:2106.13822 (2021)
7. Ladhak, F., Durmus, E., Cardie, C., McKeown, K.: Wikilingua: a new benchmark dataset for cross-lingual abstractive summarization. arXiv preprint. arXiv:2010.03093 (2020)
8. Lin, C.Y.: Rouge: a package for automatic evaluation of summaries. In: Text Summarization Branches Out, pp. 74–81. Association for Computational Linguistics, Barcelona, Spain (2004). https://aclanthology.org/W04-1013
9. Liu, Y., et al.: Multilingual denoising pre-training for neural machine translation. Trans. Assoc. Comput. Linguis. **8**, 726–742 (2020)
10. Mihalcea, R., Tarau, P.: Textrank: bringing order into text. In: Proceedings of the 2004 Conference on Empirical Methods in Natural Language Processing, pp. 404–411 (2004)
11. Nallapati, R., Zhou, B., Gulcehre, C., Xiang, B., et al.: Abstractive text summarization using sequence-to-sequence rnns and beyond. arXiv preprint. arXiv:1602.06023 (2016)
12. Narayan, S., Cohen, S.B., Lapata, M.: Don't give me the details, just the summary! topic-aware convolutional neural networks for extreme summarization. arXiv preprint. arXiv:1808.08745 (2018)
13. Nguyen, K., Daumé III, H.: Global voices: crossing borders in automatic news summarization. arXiv preprint. arXiv:1910.00421 (2019)
14. Sandhaus, E.: The New York times annotated corpus. Linguis. Data Consortium, Philadelphia **6**(12), e26752 (2008)
15. Scialom, T., Dray, P.A., Lamprier, S., Piwowarski, B., Staiano, J.: MLSUM: the multilingual summarization corpus. arXiv preprint. arXiv:2004.14900 (2020)
16. Srinivasan, K., Raman, K., Chen, J., Bendersky, M., Najork, M.: Wit: wikipedia-based image text dataset for multimodal multilingual machine learning. In: Proceedings of the 44th International ACM SIGIR Conference on Research and Development in Information Retrieval, pp. 2443–2449 (2021)
17. Wang, L., Li, Y., Aslan, O., Vinyals, O.: Wikigraphs: a wikipedia text-knowledge graph paired dataset. arXiv preprint. arXiv:2107.09556 (2021)
18. Xue, L., et al.: mt5: a massively multilingual pre-trained text-to-text transformer. arXiv preprint. arXiv:2010.11934 (2020)

Rethinking Crowd Sourcing for Semantic Similarity

Shaul Solomon[1], Adam Cohn[1], Hernan Rosenblum[1], Chezi Hershkovitz[1],
and Ivan P. Yamshchikov[2(✉)]

[1] Y-Data Tel Aviv, Tel Aviv, Israel
[2] LEYA Laboratory, Yandex and Higher School of Economics, St. Petersburg, Russia
ivan@yamshchikov.info

Abstract. Estimation of semantic similarity is crucial for various natural language processing (NLP) tasks. In the absence of a general theory of semantic information, many papers rely on human annotators as the source of ground truth for semantic similarity estimation. This paper investigates the ambiguities inherent in crowdsourced semantic labeling. It shows that annotators that treat semantic similarity as a binary category, namely, two sentences are either similar or not similar, and there is no middle ground, play the most critical role in the labeling. The paper offers heuristics to filter out unreliable annotators and stimulates further discussions on the human perception of semantics as a key to further developing human-centered artificial intelligence.

Keywords: Semantic similarity · Style transfer · Crowd sourcing

1 Introduction

Human-labeled datasets are routinely used as golden datasets for benchmarking NLP algorithms. For some NLP tasks like Part-of-Speech Tagging or Named Entity Recognition, the labeling criteria are rigorous, yet such formulations are lacking for others. Many baselines in modern NLP rely on the idea that certain aspects of natural language are understood intuitively by human annotators. This implicit assumption that semantics are definitive and unambiguous is often the only argument for ontological consistency of obtained evaluations on a given dataset. This paper demonstrates that this assumption does not hold for semantic similarity measures. It also finds that the researcher could detect unreliable annotators and thus significantly affect the labeling results via domain-specific features of the labeling process. The contributions of this paper are as follows:

- it highlights that intuitive understanding of semantic similarity varies across language speakers. In the absence of a universal unsupervised semantic similarity measure, these differences lead to the implicit noise in the research outcomes;
- using human assessment on thirty-five thousand labeled pairs of sentences the paper explores various inconsistencies present in the labeling;

V. Malykh and A. Filchenkov (Eds.): AINL 2022, CCIS 1731, pp. 70–81, 2022.
https://doi.org/10.1007/978-3-031-23372-2_7

– it proposes five possible heuristics to filter unreliable annotators and evaluates the impact of such filtering on various unsupervised semantic similarity measures.

If NLP community wants to advance human-machine text and speech interfaces, we must consider these factors. Moreover, it might be that implementing some measures of fuzzy semantics might facilitate human-machine interaction better than a current single-measure approach based on crowdsourced data.

2   Related Work

Large-scale annotated datasets (such as Treebank, Imagenet, and many others) have dramatically increased performance in many sub-fields of Machine Learning. However, they are extremely expensive and take a long time to develop. One well-established method for obtaining large-scale labeled datasets is crowdsourcing. In recent years we have seen the rise of various crowdsourcing services, which provide non-expert annotated labels. Outsourcing the labeling process to external services makes it possible to scale horizontally. Still, researchers face significant challenges to both ensure the quality of the labels and validate that the data is labeled according to the task's criteria. When dealing with non-expert annotators, the issue of quality assurance arises. Most requesters rely on redundancy (Majority Vote) or use some form of Golden Dataset to filter out unreliable annotators. Beyond the classical methods, many statistical methods have been proposed to address the issue.

Dawid & Skene [4] initially proposed an Expectation-Maximization algorithm to predict the error rate for each annotator. Many other probabilistic models have been proposed [23,29] to approximate both annotator error and bias [8], and the difficulty of particular labels and models [24]. While most of these models have been intended to be generalizable, this paper makes the argument that progress in Natural Language Understanding (NLU) requires attention to the domain-specific attributes of semantic data.

3   Domain-Specific Annotator Attributes for Natural Language

There are always two necessary elements in any form of communication or usage of language: form and meaning. When the meaning is tightly bound to the form, one can take the form context-free and be able to extract the meaning directly. However, it would be impossible to parse the intended meaning in natural language communication without some external knowledge base. The so-called *symbol grounding problem* [7] states that one can not derive the meaning of a sentence from the syntax alone. Meaning is derived from many sources, the context, the tone of voice, the relationship between interlocutors, etc.

While the NLP community has made great strides in developing a better ability to understand the syntactical distribution of a language, we have yet to make any clear headway in modeling meaning [2]. Although annotators may internally feel that they have an intuitive sense of semantic preservation, there does not seem to be a consistent agreement between people (and even for the same person in varying circumstances).

Several basic challenges cause such inconsistencies. First of all, the overlap between the form and semantics is very fuzzy, [9,26,27]; for example, given a pair of sentences in which the only distinction is the sentiment (ex: "I love pizza." vs. "I hate pizza.") human annotators agree that semantics similarity is low while some NLP researchers working on text style transfer treat sentiment as style attribute and evaluate these two sentences as semantically similar. Second, there are many possible axes upon which to calculate semantic similarity (communicative intent [28], topic identification [18], emotion recognition [5]); it is not clear how these axes rank when we are after a general measure of semantic similarity. Finally, personal characteristics of the annotator, such as implicit understanding of the context or varying background experience, systematically affect the judgment of the annotators.

4   The Data

To see differences in the semantic tendencies of human annotation, we used several standard paraphrase and style transfer datasets alongside a random selection of sentence pairs from each dataset. Similar to [30] the random pairs of sentences are used for the baseline of sentences that have no semantic overlap whatsoever. The paraphrase datasets include different versions of English Bibles [3], English Paralex dataset[1], and English Paraphrase dataset[2]. The style transfer datasets are the dataset of politeness introduced in [22] referred further as GYAFC, and Yelp! Reviews[3] enhanced with human-written reviews with opposite sentiment provided by [25].

Three independent annotators labeled every pair of sentences with a score from 1–5 (where 1 stood for two sentences being dissimilar, while 5 stood for two sentences with identical meaning). To facilitate further research of human-labeling inconsistencies for the tasks of semantic similarity, we make all collected information on the labeling process available for further study, thus enabling research transparency[4].

There are three significant sources of *noise* affecting this labeling procedure. The first sources of noise are **unreliable annotators**. These people don't give thoughtful responses and randomly fill their answers. Such annotators are present in all crowdsourcing tasks, and there are many methods to filter them out, for example, [14,15].

---

[1] http://knowitall.cs.washington.edu/paralex/.
[2] http://paraphrase.org.
[3] https://www.yelp.com/dataset.
[4] https://github.com/ShaulSolomon/Rethinking-Crowd-Sourcing-Semantic-Simila rity.

The second source of noise is the **1–5 labeling scheme** itself. On the one hand, the continuous scale from one to five presents the possibility for an annotator to mark a pair with 3, implying that two sentences are neither similar nor dissimilar. On the other hand, one could argue that by definition, the lack of similarity inherently equates to dissimilarity. We tested these two interpretations with a dozen of NLP professionals and were surprised to find out that there is no academic agreement as to which of the two scale interpretations were more appropriate.

The final source of noise could be **certain personal qualities of the annotators**. For example, certain users could be more radical in their judgment and have a preference to give extreme ratings (1,5) while others might be more moderate and give more centrist ratings (2,4), see [16].

5   Experiments

We conducted experiments to estimate the impact of these noise sources on evaluations of unsupervised semantic measures. Initially, we worked under the assumption of a minimal consistency requirement for a measure of semantic similarity, i.e., random sentences being ranked less similar than non-random sentences on average. However, when trying to validate that assumption by analyzing the similarity score distributions relative to the labels for different measures, we discovered numerous examples of low-quality labels. As a result, we strove to formalize the noise patterns into clear heuristics that can be applied to any dataset using the metadata available on a publicly available crowdsourcing platform.

One can argue that the heuristics proposed below are generalizable to any form of human judgment due to the inherent ambiguity within written language discussed prior. This is a legitimate claim, and as such, gaining a clearer picture of the biases and noise in the data becomes even more crucial for NLP tasks that require any form of human quantitative estimates. The heuristics below are by no means an exhaustive list but rather to be viewed as a sample of the myriad of factors that need to be addressed as we strive towards a more comprehensive formulation of semantic similarity.

5.1   Filtering Heuristics for Unreliable Annotators

We experimented with five different heuristics:

1. **Slow Annotators**: those whose mean labeling time is much greater than the average labeling time. We denoted the annotator with a mean labeling time greater than 300 s as a slow annotator. This places them in the 98th percentile in terms of average labeling duration in our dataset.
2. **Low Variance**: if the variance for all of the labels given by one annotator is lower than 1. This means that the vast majority of the labels are annotated with the same label by this annotator.

3. **High Random**: remove labelers whose mean semantic similarity score of all random pairs is higher than their mean semantic similarity score for non-random pairs. The random pairs have to score lower than the semantically similar ones among reliable annotators.

4. **Disagreeable Annotators**: using reduced labeling (Scores below 3 collapse into -1, 3 becomes 0, and anything above 3 collapses into 1) we filter any annotator who happens to disagree with an unanimous decision from the other two annotators more than in half of the cases.

5. **Sentimentally Dis-aligned Annotators**: as discussed earlier, the relationship between sentiment and semantics is ambiguous, so we wanted to filter out annotators who used the sentiment to determine semantics inconsistently.[5]

If the annotator corresponds to one of these categories we pronounce this annotator to be unreliable. To make our experiments clear and reproducible, we publish the source code, with the specification of all dependencies, including external libraries (See footnote 4).

5.2 Correlation with Automated Semantic Similarity Metrics

We took ten of the most used metrics for content preservation and semantic similarity to estimate how the labeling noise can interfere with the NLP benchmarks that use semantic similarity measurements. **Word overlap** is calculated as a percentage of words that occur in both texts. **chrF** [21] is a character n-gram F-score that measures number of n-grams that coincide in input and output. **Cosine similarity** is calculated in line with [6] either with pre-trained GloVe [19] or FastText word embeddings [10]. **POS-distance** looks for nouns in the input and output and is calculated as a pairwise distance between the embeddings of the found nouns. **L2 distance** between Elmo [20] embeddings of two sentences. **WMD** [11] defines the distance between two documents as an optimal transport problem between the embedded words. **BLEU** [17] is one of the most common semantic similarity measures. **ROUGE** [12] compares any text to any other (typically human-generated) summary using a recall-oriented approach and unigrams, with bi-grams, and [13] with the longest co-occurring n-grams in sequence. **Meteor** [1] metric is based on a harmonic mean of unigram precision and recall, with recall weighted higher than precision and some additional features, such as stemming and synonymy matching. Finally, **BERT score** proposed in [31] is a BERT-based estimator of semantic similarity between two pieces of text.

---

[5] Taking pairs which have a very high word overlap (BLUE score over 0.8) - indicating nearly identical syntactical content - but with sentiment score differences ≥ 1.9 (using huggingface's sentiment-analysis pipeline is bound by $[-1,1]$), we filter out annotators whose labeling variance on those pairs was greater than 1.

Table 1. The Baseline correlation and the impact of each of the heuristics for each of the metrics. [1]—slow annotators, [2]—low variance, [3]—high random, [4]—disagreeable annotators, [5]—sentimentally dis-aligned annotators

Corr.	Bleu	Bleu1	Glove	Fasttext	BertScore	chrfScore	POS Dist. score
baseline	0.41	0.60	0.45	0.51	0.59	0.58	0.35
[1]	0.39 (−4%)	0.58 (−3%)	0.44 (−3%)	0.49 (−3%)	0.57 (−4%)	0.56 (−4%)	0.34 (−4%)
[2]	0.44 (+7%)	0.65 (+8%)	0.48 (+5%)	0.53 (+5%)	0.64 (+8%)	0.63 (+7%)	0.38 (+8%)
[3]	0.43 (+4%)	0.63 (+4%)	0.47 (+3%)	0.53 (+3%)	0.62 (+4%)	0.61 (+4%)	0.36 (+4%)
[4]	0.41	0.60	0.45	0.51	0.59	0.58	0.35
[5]	0.38 (−9%)	0.54 (−9%)	0.41 (−10%)	0.45 (−10%)	0.54 (−9%)	0.53 (−9%)	0.31 (−10%)
[1, 2]	0.43 (+5%)	0.64 (+6%)	0.47 (+4%)	0.52 (+3%)	0.63 (+6%)	0.61 (+5%)	0.37 (+6%)
[1, 3]	0.41	0.61 (+1%)	0.46 (+1%)	0.51	0.60 (+1%)	0.59 (+1%)	0.35
[1, 4]	0.39 (−4%)	0.58 (−4%)	0.44 (−3%)	0.49 (−3%)	0.57 (−3%)	0.56 (−3%)	0.34 (−4%)
[1, 5]	0.36 (−12%)	0.53 (−12%)	0.40 (−12%)	0.44 (−12%)	0.52 (−11%)	0.51 (−11%)	0.30 (−13%)
[2, 3]	**0.45 (+11%)**	**0.67 (+11%)**	**0.49 (+9%)**	**0.55 (+8%)**	**0.66 (+11%)**	**0.64 (+10%)**	**0.39 (+11%)**
[2, 4]	0.44 (+7%)	0.65 (+8%)	0.48 (+6%)	0.53 (+5%)	0.64 (+8%)	0.63 (+7%)	0.38 (+8%)
[2, 5]	0.44 (+8%)	0.64 (+6%)	0.46 (+2%)	0.51	0.63 (+6%)	0.62 (+6%)	0.37 (+6%)
[3, 4]	0.43 (+4%)	0.63 (+4%)	0.47 (+4%)	0.53 (+3%)	0.62 (+4%)	0.61 (+4%)	0.36 (+4%)
[3, 5]	0.40 (−3%)	0.58 (−4%)	0.43 (−6%)	0.48 (−6%)	0.57 (−4%)	0.56 (−5%)	0.33 (−6%)
[4, 5]	0.38 (−9%)	0.54 (−10%)	0.41 (−10%)	0.45 (−11%)	0.54 (−9%)	0.53 (−9%)	0.31 (−11%)
[1, 2, 3]	0.45 (+9%)	0.66 (+10%)	0.49 (+8%)	0.54 (+7%)	0.65 (+10%)	0.64 (+9%)	0.38 (+9%)
[1, 2, 4]	0.43 (+5%)	0.64 (+6%)	0.47 (+4%)	0.52 (+3%)	0.63 (+6%)	0.61 (+5%)	0.37 (+6%)
[1, 2, 5]	0.44 (+8%)	0.64 (+6%)	0.46 (+2%)	0.52 (+2%)	0.63 (+6%)	0.61 (+5%)	0.37 (+6%)
[1, 3, 4]	0.41	0.61 (+1%)	0.46 (+1%)	0.51	0.60 (+1%)	0.59 (+1%)	0.35
[1, 3, 5]	0.39 (−5%)	0.57 (−6%)	0.42 (−7%)	0.47 (−8%)	0.56 (−6%)	0.55 (−6%)	0.32 (−9%)
[1, 4, 5]	0.36 (−11%)	0.53 (−12%)	0.40 (−12%)	0.44 (−13%)	0.52 (−12%)	0.51 (−12%)	0.30 (−14%)
[2, 3, 4]	**0.45 (+11%)**	**0.67 (+11%)**	**0.49 (+9%)**	**0.55 (+8%)**	**0.66 (+11%)**	**0.64 (+10%)**	**0.39 (+11%)**
[2, 3, 5]	0.45 (+9%)	0.65 (+8%)	0.47 (+4%)	0.52 (+3%)	0.64 (+8%)	0.63 (+7%)	0.38 (+7%)
[2, 4, 5]	0.44 (+8%)	0.64 (+6%)	0.46 (+2%)	0.51	0.63 (+6%)	0.62 (+6%)	0.37 (+6%)
[3, 4, 5]	0.40 (−3%)	0.58 (−4%)	0.43 (−6%)	0.48 (−6%)	0.57 (−4%)	0.56 (−5%)	0.33 (−6%)
[1, 2, 3, 4]	0.45 (+9%)	0.66 (+10%)	0.49 (+8%)	0.54 (+7%)	0.65 (+10%)	0.64 (+9%)	0.38 (+9%)
[1, 2, 3, 5]	0.45 (+9%)	0.65 (+8%)	0.48 (+5%)	0.52 (+2%)	0.64 (+9%)	0.63 (+7%)	0.38 (+7%)
[1, 2, 4, 5]	0.44 (+7%)	0.64 (+5%)	0.46 (+2%)	0.51	0.64 (+9%)	0.61 (+5%)	0.37 (+5%)
[1, 3, 4, 5]	0.39 (−5%)	0.57 (−6%)	0.42 (−7%)	0.47 (−8%)	0.56 (−6%)	0.55 (−6%)	0.32 (−9%)
[2, 3, 4, 5]	0.45 (+9%)	0.65 (+8%)	0.47 (+5%)	0.52 (+3%)	0.64 (+8%)	0.63 (+7%)	0.38 (+7%)
[1, 2, 3, 4, 5]	0.45 (+9%)	0.65 (+8%)	0.48 (+5%)	0.52 (+2%)	0.64 (+9%)	0.63 (+7%)	0.38 (+7%)

Table 2. The Baseline correlation and the impact of each of the heuristics for each of the metrics. [1]—slow annotators, [2]—low variance, [3]—high random, [4]—disagreeable annotators, [5]—sentimentally dis-aligned annotators

	ROUGE-1	ROUGE-2	ROUGE-1	L2 score	WMD	1-gram overlap
Base correlation	0.61	0.53	0.60	0.56	0.50	0.59
[1]	0.59 (−4%)	0.51 (−4%)	0.58 (−4%)	0.54 (−3%)	0.48 (−3%)	0.57 (−4%)
[2]	0.66 (+8%)	0.57 (+7%)	0.65 (+8%)	0.60 (+7%)	0.53 (+7%)	0.63 (+8%)
[3]	0.63 (+4%)	0.55 (+4%)	0.62 (+4%)	0.59 (+4%)	0.52 (+4%)	0.61 (+4%)
[4]	0.61	0.53	0.60	0.56	0.50	0.59
[5]	0.55 (−10%)	0.48 v9%)	0.54 (−10%)	0.51 (−10%)	0.45 (−10%)	0.53 (−10%)
[1, 2]	0.65 (+6%)	0.56 (+5%)	0.64 (+6%)	0.59 (+5%)	0.52 (+5%)	0.62 (+6%)
[1, 3]	0.62 (+1%)	0.53 (+1%)	0.61 (+1%)	0.57 (+2%)	0.51 (+1%)	0.59 (+1%)
[1, 4]	0.59 (−4%)	0.51 (−4%)	0.58 (−4%)	0.54 (−3%)	0.48 (−3%)	0.57 (−4%)
[1, 5]	0.53 (−12%)	0.47 (−12%)	0.53 (−12%)	0.50 (−12%)	0.44 (−13%)	0.52 (−12%)
[2, 3]	0.68 (+11%)	0.59 (+10%)	0.67 (+11%)	0.62 (+10%)	0.55 (+10%)	0.65 (+11%)
[2, 4]	0.66 (+8%)	0.57 (+7%)	0.65 (+8%)	0.60 (+7%)	0.53 (+7%)	0.63 (+8%)
[2, 5]	0.64 (+5%)	0.57 (+7%)	0.64 (+6%)	0.59 (+4%)	0.51 (+3%)	0.62 (+6%)
[3, 4]	0.63 (+4%)	0.55 (+4%)	0.62 (+4%)	0.59 (+4%)	0.52 (+4%)	0.61 (+4%)
[3, 5]	0.58 (−5%)	0.51 (−4%)	0.57 (−4%)	0.54 (−5%)	0.47 (−5%)	0.56 (−4%)
[4, 5]	0.55 (−10%)	0.48 (−9%)	0.54 (−10%)	0.51 (−10%)	0.45 (−11%)	0.53 (−10%)
[1, 2, 3]	0.67 (+10%)	0.58 (+9%)	0.66 (+10%)	0.61 (+9%)	0.54 (+9%)	0.65 (+10%)
[1, 2, 4]	0.65 (+6%)	0.56 (+5%)	0.64 (+6%)	0.59 (+6%)	0.52 (+5%)	0.62 (+6%)
[1, 2, 5]	0.64 (+5%)	0.56 (+6%)	0.64 (+6%)	0.59 (+4%)	0.51 (+3%)	0.62 (+6%)
[1, 3, 4]	0.62 (+1%)	0.53 (+1%)	0.61 (+1%)	0.57 (+2%)	0.51 (+1%)	0.59 (+1%)
[1, 3, 5]	0.57 (−6%)	0.50 (−6%)	0.57 (−6%)	0.53 (−6%)	0.46 (−7%)	0.55 (−6%)
[1, 4, 5]	0.54 (−12%)	0.47 (−11%)	0.53 (−12%)	0.50 (−12%)	0.44 (−13%)	0.52 (−12%)
[2, 3, 4]	**0.68 (+11%)**	**0.59 (+10%)**	**0.67 (+11%)**	**0.62 (+10%)**	**0.55 (+10%)**	**0.65 (+11%)**
[2, 3, 5]	0.66 (+7%)	0.58 (+9%)	0.65 (+8%)	0.60 (+7%)	0.52 (+5%)	0.64 (+8%)
[2, 4, 5]	0.64 (+5%)	0.57 (+7%)	0.64 (+6%)	0.59 (+4%)	0.51 (+3%)	0.62 (+6%)
[3, 4, 5]	0.58 (−5%)	0.51 (−4%)	0.57 (−4%)	0.54 (−4%)	0.47 (−5%)	0.56 (−4%)
[1, 2, 3, 4]	0.67 (+10%)	0.58 (+9%)	0.66 (+10%)	0.61 (+9%)	0.54 (+9%)	0.65 (+10%)
[1, 2, 3, 5]	0.66 (+8%)	0.58 (+8%)	0.65 (+8%)	0.60 (+7%)	0.52 (+4%)	0.64 (+8%)
[1, 2, 4, 5]	0.64 (+5%)	0.56 (+6%)	0.64 (+6%)	0.59 (+4%)	0.51 (+2%)	0.62 (+6%)
[1, 3, 4, 5]	0.57 (−6%)	0.50 (−6%)	0.57 (−6%)	0.53 (−6%)	0.46 (−7%)	0.55 (−6%)
[2, 3, 4, 5]	0.66 (+8%)	0.58 (+9%)	0.65 (+8%)	0.60 (+7%)	0.52 (+5%)	0.64 (+8%)
[1, 2, 3, 4, 5]	0.66 (+8%)	0.58 (+8%)	0.65 (+8%)	0.60 (+7%)	0.52 (+4%)	0.64 (+8%)

Table 3. The correlation between automated semantic similarity metrics and the human labels over all datasets, and the same correlation when unreliable annotators are filtered out. The automated metrics improve from 2 to 9 percentage points depending on the metric.

Metric	Baseline correlation	Filtered heuristics	Percentage increase
ROUGE-1	0.61	0.65	7.6%
bleu1	0.60	0.65	7.9%
ROUGE-l	0.60	0.65	8.0%
BertScore	0.59	0.64	8.5%
1-gram_overlap	0.59	0.64	8.0%
chrfScore	0.58	0.63	7.3%
L2_score	0.56	0.6	6.6%
ROUGE-2	0.53	0.58	8.4%
fasttext_cosine	0.51	0.52	2.2%
WMD	0.5	0.52	4.4%
glove_cosine	0.45	0.48	4.6%
bleu	0.41	0.45	9.0%
POS Dist score	0.35	0.38	7.2%

Table 3 shows how the automated semantic similarity metrics correlate with human labels and how they correlate after we filter unreliable annotators defined according to the heuristics above. Tables 1 – 2 show the resulting experiments with all five heuristics and relative changes in correlation between human labeling and unsupervised semantic similarity metrics depending on the filtering procedure.

The results clearly demonstrate that relatively straightforward filtering of human labels could add or subtract up to *eleven* percentage points to the results of an automated evaluation. This is disturbing since far more minor changes in performance are commonly regarded as improvements in some NLP tasks.

In all our experiments situations we see that the combination of **Low Variance** and **High Random** filtering heuristics has the strongest impact on the correlation with automated evaluation methods. Under certain circumstances, heuristics based on **Disagreeable Labelers** and **Sentimentally Dis-aligned Labelers** also increase the correlation. On the other hand, filtering **Slow Annotators** out only hurts the performance.

Table 4 shows a more nuanced picture of correlations between the automated metrics and the labels of different annotators. We denote those annotators who selected {1,5} over 50% of the time as *Radical* and those who selected {2,4} as *Centrist*; the label 3 was ignored in calculations of these criteria, and only annotators with variance above 1 were included. Comparing results in Table 3 and Table 4 one could see that radical annotators play a major part in the resulting

Table 4. The Baseline correlation without filtering and the improvement after filtering unreliable annotators for Radical and Centrist Annotators independently.

	Radicals		Centrists	
	Baseline	Filtered	Baseline	Filtered
ROUGE-1	0.70	0.70	0.28	0.45
bleu1	0.69	0.69	0.28	0.46
ROUGE-l	0.69	0.69	0.28	0.46
BertScore	0.69	0.69	0.28	0.46
1-gram_overlap	0.68	0.68	0.28	0.45
chrfScore	0.67	0.67	0.28	0.44
L2_score	0.64	0.65	0.25	0.39
ROUGE-2	0.61	0.61	0.26	0.41
fasttext_cosine	0.57	0.57	0.21	0.32
WMD	0.57	0.56	0.21	0.33
glove_cosine	0.51	0.51	0.19	0.23
bleu	0.47	0.48	0.21	0.32
POS Dist score	0.41	0.40	0.16	0.28

overall correlations between human labels and automated semantic similarity metrics. Moreover, filtering unreliable annotators only affects correlations of the labels given by Centrists. This either shows that treating semantic similarity as a binary value when using crowdsourced human labels might be beneficial for less ambiguous results or hints that current unsupervised metrics of semantic similarity have a hard time capturing nuance that some human annotators see.

6   Discussion

Constant attempts of the NLP research community to formalize certain aspects of natural language are significant. Yet, in the case of semantic similarity measures sourced from a crowd, these efforts might hinder the progress towards more "relatable" natural language models. Some level of ambivalence in a language might be its' feature rather than a bug. As we discussed the design of the labeling among ourselves and other professionals in the NLP community, there are two distinct "cultures". Some annotators treat the scale uniformly. These annotators treat lower labels as corresponding to a lower degree of similarity while using bigger labels to denote higher semantic similarity. Other annotators interpret the middle of the scale as neither similar nor opposing examples. They regard the lower half of the scale as a negative semantic relation between two texts while treating the upper half of the scale as a similarity metric. One could also clearly contrast "radical" annotators and those who were less sure in their judgment. Such factors could not only be the source of error for NLP research but also might be insights into how a "human-friendly" natural language interface could behave and what personalization dimensions it could have. For example, a sub-task with a Semantic-based NLP model could be to determine what type of similarity the user intended.

7 Conclusion

This paper attempts to quantify the inherent ambiguity prevalent in any NLP task that relies on human judgment as a measure of semantic similarity. It demonstrates that a simple heuristic curation of human annotation could give up to **eleven extra percentage points** in terms of the model performance estimated with some unsupervised semantic similarity measure.

The series of experiments conducted in the paper provides several rules of thumb to reduce the ambiguity of human labels:

- when labeling treat semantic similarity as a binary feature asking if two texts are similar or not;
- add sentence pairs where there is no semantic similarity whatsoever and filter unreliable annotators that make mistakes on these pairs;
- majority vote improves the consistency of your data but it is not as good, and drastic, as filtering out annotators with a low variance of labels and annotators that systematically miss the right answer on clearly dissimilar sentence pairs.

The paper also explores dividing annotators between *Radical* and *Centrists*, both as a way to increase correlation and in reducing the ambiguity within Semantic Similarity labeling.

Acknowledgements. This work is an output of a research project implemented as part of the Basic Research Program at the National Research University Higher School of Economics (HSE University).

The research was supported with a crows-sourcing grant from Toloka (https://toloka.ai/).

References

1. Banerjee, S., Lavie, A.: Meteor: an automatic metric for MT evaluation with improved correlation with human judgments. In: Proceedings of the ACL Workshop on Intrinsic and Extrinsic Evaluation Measures for Machine Translation and/or Summarization, pp. 65–72 (2005)
2. Bender, E.M., Koller, A.: Climbing towards NLU: on meaning, form, and understanding in the age of data. In: ACL (2020)
3. Carlson, K., Riddell, A., Rockmore, D.: Zero-shot style transfer in text using recurrent neural networks. arXiv preprint. arXiv:1711.04731 (2017)
4. Dawid, A.P., Skene, A.: Maximum likelihood estimation of observer error-rates using the EM algorithm. J. Royal Stat. Soc. Series C-Appl. Stat. **28**, 20–28 (1979)
5. Franzoni, V., Milani, A., Biondi, G.: SEMO: a semantic model for emotion recognition in web objects. In: Proceedings of the International Conference on Web Intelligence, pp. 953–958 (2017)

6. Fu, Z., Tan, X., Peng, N., Zhao, D., Yan, R.: Style transfer in text: exploration and evaluation. In: AAAI (2018)
7. Harnad, S.: The symbol grounding problem. Physica D **42**(1–3), 335–346 (1990)
8. Ipeirotis, P.G., Provost, F., Wang, J.: Quality management on amazon mechanical turk. In: HCOMP '10 (2010)
9. Jafaritazehjani, S., Lecorvé, G., Lolive, D., Kelleher, J.: Style versus content: A distinction without a (learnable) difference? In: Proceedings of the 28th International Conference on Computational Linguistics, pp. 2169–2180 (2020)
10. Joulin, A., Grave, E., Bojanowski, P., Douze, M., Jégou, H., Mikolov, T.: Fasttext. zip: compressing text classification models. arXiv preprint. arXiv:1612.03651 (2016)
11. Kusner, M., Sun, Y., Kolkin, N., Weinberger, K.: From word embeddings to document distances. In: International Conference on Machine Learning, pp. 957–966 (2015)
12. Lin, C.Y., Hovy, E.: The automated acquisition of topic signatures for text summarization. In: Proceedings of the 18th Conference on Computational Linguistics-Vol. 1, pp. 495–501. Association for Computational Linguistics (2000)
13. Lin, C.Y., Och, F.J.: Automatic evaluation of machine translation quality using longest common subsequence and skip-bigram statistics. In: Proceedings of the 42nd Annual Meeting on Association for Computational Linguistics, p. 605. Association for Computational Linguistics (2004)
14. Lofi, C.: Just ask a human? - controlling quality in relational similarity and analogy processing using the crowd. In: BTW Workshops (2013)
15. Oleson, D., Sorokin, A., Laughlin, G., Hester, V., Le, J., Biewald, L.: Programmatic gold: targeted and scalable quality assurance in crowdsourcing. In: Proceedings of the 11th AAAI Conference on Human Computation, AAAIWS'11-11, p. 43–48. AAAI Press (2011)
16. Panda, S.K., Bhoi, S.K., Singh, M.: A collaborative filtering recommendation algorithm based on normalization approach. J. Ambient Intell. Humanized Comput. **11**(11), 4643–4665 (2020). https://doi.org/10.1007/s12652-020-01711-x
17. Papineni, K., Roukos, S., Ward, T., Zhu, W.J.: Bleu: a method for automatic evaluation of machine translation. In: Proceedings of the 40th Annual Meeting on Association for Computational Linguistics, pp. 311–318. Association for Computational Linguistics (2002)
18. Peinelt, N., Nguyen, D., Liakata, M.: tBERT: topic models and BERT joining forces for semantic similarity detection. In: Proceedings of the 58th Annual Meeting of the Association for Computational Linguistics, pp. 7047–7055 (2020)
19. Pennington, J., Socher, R., Manning, C.: Glove: global vectors for word representation. In: Proceedings of the 2014 Conference on Empirical Methods in Natural Language Processing (EMNLP), pp. 1532–1543 (2014)
20. Peters, M.E., et al.: Deep contextualized word representations. arXiv preprint. arXiv:1802.05365 (2018)
21. Popović, M.: chrF: character n-gram F-score for automatic MT evaluation. In: Proceedings of the 10th Workshop on Statistical Machine Translation, pp. 392–395 (2015)
22. Rao, S., Tetreault, J.: Dear sir or madam, may i introduce the GYAFC dataset: corpus, benchmarks and metrics for formality style transfer. arXiv preprint. arXiv:1803.06535 (2018)
23. Raykar, V.C., et al.: Learning from crowds. J. Mach. Learn. Res. **11**, 1297–1322 (2010)

24. Sheng, V., Provost, F., Ipeirotis, P.G.: Get another label? improving data quality and data mining using multiple, noisy labelers. Data Collection & Data Estimation Methodology eJournal, Econometrics (2008)
25. Tian, Y., Hu, Z., Yu, Z.: Structured content preservation for unsupervised text style transfer. In: arXiv preprint (2018). https://arxiv.org/pdf/1810.06526.pdf
26. Tikhonov, A., Shibaev, V., Nagaev, A., Nugmanova, A., Yamshchikov, I.P.: Style transfer for texts: retrain, report errors, compare with rewrites. In: Proceedings of the 2019 Conference on Empirical Methods in Natural Language Processing and the 9th International Joint Conference on Natural Language Processing (EMNLP-IJCNLP), pp. 3927–3936 (2019)
27. Tikhonov, A., Yamshchikov, I.P.: What is wrong with style transfer for texts? arXiv preprint. arXiv:1808.04365 (2018)
28. Westera, M., Boleda, G.: Don't blame distributional semantics if it can't do entailment. In: Proceedings of the 13th International Conference on Computational Semantics-Long Papers, pp. 120–133 (2019)
29. Whitehill, J., Ruvolo, P., Wu, T., Bergsma, J., Movellan, J.: Whose vote should count more: optimal integration of labels from labelers of unknown expertise. In: NIPS (2009)
30. Yamshchikov, I.P., Shibaev, V., Khlebnikov, N., Tikhonov, A.: Style-transfer and paraphrase: Looking for a sensible semantic similarity metric. In: Proceedings of the AAAI Conference on Artificial Intelligence. vol. 35, pp. 14213–14220 (2021)
31. Zhang, T., Kishore, V., Wu, F., Weinberger, K.Q., Artzi, Y.: Bertscore: evaluating text generation with bert. arXiv preprint. arXiv:1904.09675 (2019)

Interplay of Visual and Acoustic Cues of Irony Perception: A Case Study of Actor's Speech

Uliana Kochetkova(✉) 🆔, Vera Evdokimova 🆔, Pavel Skrelin 🆔, Rada German 🆔,
and Daria Novoselova 🆔

Saint Petersburg University, Saint Petersburg 199034, Russia
{u.kochetkova,v.evdokimova,p.skrelin}@spbu.ru, {st067973,
st065112}@student.spbu.ru

Abstract. This paper deals with the interaction of visual and acoustic cues of irony, observed in the speech of Russian professional actors. We selected ironic and non-ironic utterances from modern films and series taking into account narrow and broad context, lexical and semantic markers. Then we extracted the target utterances from the context eliminating any markers of irony. The participants of the perceptual experiments could rely only on the visual and acoustic (prosodic) cues. In the first experiment we suggested to the participants mute video files containing the target ironic and non-ironic utterances. The second experiment was conducted with the audio files only of the same utterances extracted from the films. In the third experiment video and audio were suggested simultaneously, as in the natural situation of film watching, but still without any context or lexical marker. Segment duration, pitch movement, gestures and mimics, as well as their synchrony in the well-recognized target utterances were analyzed. The results of the experiments demonstrated that the visual cues were more important for irony perception than the audio signal. Yet, some video stimuli that had low recognition of irony were better recognized in the experiment with audio. It led us to suppose that actors use in various proportion visual and acoustic cues to express irony in speech. The results of this research can have practical application in both speech recognition and speech generation used in artificial intelligence systems, as well as in the forensic phonetics and second language acquisition.

Keywords: Verbal irony · Antiphrasis · Actors' Speech · Acoustic cues · Gestures · Phonetics · Pitch movement

1 Introduction

Nowadays, in the era of digital technology development, requiring the use of various information transmission channels, one of the most challenging questions of current interest is the multimodal behavior of speaker and the results of a multichannel speech perception by a listener. Despite the great variety of studies on the multimodality [1–7], neither the interaction of various information channels and modes, nor the impact of each of them on speech perception are fully understood. The increasing interest in this domain is also explained by the needs of natural animation of conversational agents in speech and video dialogue systems [8]. Another key point in modern linguistics, cognitive and artificial intelligence (AI) studies is to understand subtle features of meaning in human speech. It is still a challenge for recognition systems. Their enhancement will be possible only after a comprehensive description of various cues of speech modalities in speech perception and generation has been obtained.

One of the modalities, which is important for the correct interpretation of the message is the irony, especially the antiphrasis (irony as negation). This type of verbal irony is traditionally defined as a mode of speech in which one says something different from or the opposite of what is really implied [9]. This complex phenomenon can be manifested by various means at all levels of communication, including phonetics, gestures and mimics.

To date, relatively little work has been done that examined phonetic properties of irony in Russian. Although numerous studies considered this phenomenon, most of them focused on lexical, grammatical or semantic aspects of irony. A comprehensive study of acoustic cues of irony in Russian is yet to be conducted. In our previous research we observed using the laboratory speech that the stressed vowel lengthening seems to be one of the prosodic features of irony [10, 11], as well as the increased intensity and pitch range. It correlates well with the data obtained in earlier research on English and German material [12, 13] and with some results obtained for Chinese language [14].

Thus, in the current study we aim to analyze various acoustic and visual cues of irony in speech of Russian professional actors in films and series. Moreover, we try to consider the interference and impact of each of the channels on the perception of the compound signal (video with audio). We considered gestures and mimics co-occurring with the nucleus of the phrase, comparing the direction of the gestures and of the pitch movement.

2 Material

Our research is based on the modern Russian films and series presented in open sources. During the semantic analysis accomplished by expert linguists, we selected audiovisual snippets containing ironic and non-ironic utterances from cues of both male and female actors.

2.1 Linguistic Analysis

To establish the presence or absence of irony-negation (antiphrasis) we considered the narrow and broad context, lexical and semantic markers, as well as remarks. The examples are given below.

Narrow Context. The verbal or non-verbal context, in which an utterance occurred, often helped to define unambiguously whether the utterance was pronounced with irony, notably with irony-negation, or not. For example, the utterance "Ну спасибо!" (*Oh, thanks!*) was pronounced by a character after his colleague announced about a big mistake he had made. Thus the utterance expressed displeasure instead of gratitude. Also the discourse marker – the particle "ну" (*oh, well, yeah*) – enhanced the ironic meaning.

Lexical and Semantic Markers. One example of a lexical marker has been given above (the particle "ну" (*oh, well, yeah*)). Although most discourse markers are polysemic, their concrete meaning is always clearly defined by the context and situation. Besides that, their occurrence in ironic utterances is more frequent than in the non-ironic ones. Among discourse markers, there are also few that are used only in ironic utterances, like the marker "Тоже мне" (*Some…*) or "Да ладно"(*Come on*). All such markers accompany the target utterance and reinforce the ironic meaning.

Remarks. Various remarks are typical for fiction, but they can occur in films and series as well. For example, during the dialogue, when the first character pronounces an utterance "Бедненький!" (*Poor him!*), the second replies "А откуда столько сарказма?" (*Why are you so sarcastic?*).

Broad Context. The utterance "Вот это сырники?!" (*Are these cheese pancakes?*) is a good illustration of ironic meaning revealed through the storyline. This utterance is pronounced by a mother-in-law who can't stand her daughter-in-law and constantly bullies the latter. At the same time, it includes the discourse marker – the demonstrative particle "вот" (here, this,…etc.), which amplifies the expressed emotions. Here this particle amplifies the ironic meaning.

2.2 Requirements for the Audiovisual Material

In the audiovisual material, there shouldn't be any close-ups or overlaps. One character should pronounce one utterance in one frame (utterance). The whole utterance should be pronounced without changing place or regrouping.

In order to avoid the influence of the previous knowledge of the film on the experiment participants, no famous films or quotes from such films were chosen.

3 Perceptual Experiments

The snippets from the video sources (films and series) mentioned in the previous section were presented to Russian native speakers in order to test whether they were able to identify ironic or non-ironic meaning of the stimuli. Short snippets were manually extracted from the obtained audiovisual signal in a way that did not allow for any indication of the ironic context (irony markers and explicit remarks) or non-ironic context.

A series of perceptual experiments was conducted, the first one containing muted video recordings, the second one containing corresponding audio recordings and the third one containing the same video recordings with the sound on. Each questionnaire consisted of 38 questions, 35 of which were aimed at recognition of the target phrases and three questions were asked in order to collect the personal data of the informants (their gender, age and level of Russian language competence). Since the three sets of stimuli were related, the same questions were used for the same target phrases.

The participants were instructed to play the recording (a visual in the first experiment, an audial in the second experiment and an audiovisual stimulus in the third experiment) and relate it to the sentence or the dialogue it was extracted from in written form. All the questions had 3 options: an ironic context, a non-ironic context, and the "unsure" option. The given options were devoid of any explicit indication of the ironic meaning of an utterance. This was intended to make certain that the participants were not aware of the goal of the experiment. The auditors could only choose one response option. An example of the questionnaire used in visual and audiovisual perceptual experiments is given below (Fig. 1). In the auditory experiment, the same questionnaire was given, but there were no video, only the corresponding audio files were suggested.

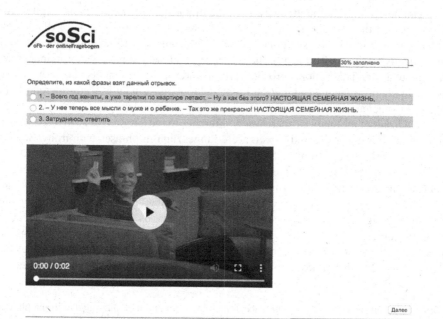

Fig. 1. An example of the questionnaire for the experiment with the mute video and the audiovisual experiment presented on the platform SoSciSurvey.de. (1)– They've been married for only one year, yet the plates are already flying all around the apartment. – Why not? A real family life; (2) – All her thoughts are now about her husband and her child. – This is great! A real family life; (3) Unsure.

The link to the survey was distributed online using the SoSci Survey platform. Each test took approximately 10–15 min to complete. An effort was made to ensure that the participants would get acquainted to only one set of data in order to avoid overlapping of the different types of stimuli.

At the time the results were collected, 31 people completed the questionnaire that presented muted video recordings, 25 people took part in the second survey containing corresponding audio fragments and 46 auditors participated in the third experiment that included audiovisual stimuli. Only participants who filled out the personal data form were considered in the study. All of the listeners who took part in the three perceptual experiments were native Russian speakers.

4 Acoustic Analysis

Audio and video recordings were processed in three programs: PRAAT, Wave Assistant and Elan. In the PRAAT program, the recordings were segmented into stressed and unstressed vowels and consonants. Then, using the script, data on the duration and intensity of each sound and of the entire phrase were obtained. In the Elan program, the segmentation was synchronized with the video to further correlate the results of the acoustic analysis with the video stream. In the Wave Assistant program, the pitch was annotated for subsequent analysis of the melodic range and to plot the pitch contour. Data on the melodic range of phrase, stressed vowel and stressed syllable were calculated in both Hz and semitones. Overall, 20 ironic and 15 neutral fragments were acoustically analyzed. The fact of the presence of additional prosodic prominence was taken into account. Additional prosodic prominence occurs when there is more than one perceptually prominent word. Furthermore, the tone movement was considered: falling and rising nucleus.

As a result of the analysis, there was a difference in the duration of unstressed vowels: in neutral phrases, unstressed vowels were longer than in phrases with irony. Stressed vowels were longer in ironic utterances than in neutral ones. However, to clarify the significance of the results obtained, a statistical analysis (Student's t-test) of the acoustic data was conducted: duration (nucleus, unstressed and stressed vowels), intensity and melodic range (phrase, stressed vowel and stressed syllable). It turned out that the only statistically significant difference between ironic phrases and non-ironic ones at the acoustic level was the melodic range in the stressed syllable. In ironic phrases, the melodic range is statistically confirmed to be greater than that of neutral phrases (see Tables 1 and 2). The values of the melodic range are given in Hertz and semitones.

Table 1. Additional prosodic prominence, tone movement and melodic range in ironic phrases.

Text of the fragment	Additional prosodic prominence	Tone movement	Melodic range in the stressed Syllable, Hz (ST)
Ха-ха (*Ha-ha*)	–	\	35 (3)
Гениально (*Genius*)	–	\	80 (8)
Сейчас (*Now*)	–	\	29 (2)
Счастливая семейная жизнь (*Happy family life*)	+	\	81 (9)
Ну это мне совершенно необходимо (*This is absolutely necessary for me*)	+	\	5 (1)

(continued)

Table 1. (*continued*)

Text of the fragment	Additional prosodic prominence	Tone movement	Melodic range in the stressed Syllable, Hz (ST)
Благородно (*That's precious*)	–	\	85 (11)
Настоящая семейная жизнь (*<It's> the real married life*)	–	\	185 (15)
Это сенсация (*It's a sensation*)	–	\	17 (2)
Похвально (*<it's commendable*)	–	\	45 (6)
Ну спасибо (*Oh, thanks*)	+	\	47 (5)
Спасибо тебе нечеловеческое (*Thank you so much*)	+	\	10 (2)
Серьезное дело у нас тут (*This is actually a serious matter*)	+	\	42 (5)
Лечиться значит (*Well, <he's> been treated*)	–	\	33 (2)
Очень смешно (*Very funny*)	+	\	16 (3)
Бедненький (*Poor*)	–	\	80 (5)
Молодец (*Well done*)	–	\	16 (3)
Да (*Yes*)	–	\	70 (10)
Вот это сырники (*Are these cheese pancakes?*)	+	/	113 (10)
Да неужели (*Really*)	+	\	58 (15)
Делать мне нечего (*I've nothing to do*)	+	\	14 (1)

Moreover, the acoustic characteristics of fragments reliably identified in the perceptual experiment with and without irony (>80% of the auditors in the experiment with sound) were analyzed separately, the same results were obtained: in fragments with irony, the stressed syllable has a greater melodic range than in neutral fragments (see Fig. 2).

One explanation for why a statistically significant difference was found only in the melodic range is that the fragments analyzed as neutral might turn out not to be quite so. Since the speakers were the actors playing the role, it was likely that their speech was

Table 2. Additional prosodic prominence, tone movement and melodic range in non-ironic phrases.

Text of the fragment	Additional prosodic prominence	Tone movement in the stressed syllable	Melodic range in the stressed syllable, Hz (ST)
Благодарю (Thank you)	–	/	14 (1)
Всенепременно (Indubitably)	–	/	36 (5)
Да, благодарю (Yes, thank you)	+	\	51 (7)
Кого (Whom)	–	\	143 (10)
Ну и кому же лететь как не Володе (Who else will fly if not Volodya)	+	\	39 (3)
Олег – это водитель (Oleg is the driver)	+	\	34 (5)
Отлично (Great)	–	\	38 (3)
Очень (Very much)	–	\	12 (1)
Понятно (<It's> clear)	–	\	15 (3)
Привет (Hello)	–	\	17 (2)
Славная девочка (<She's> a nice girl)	+	\	14 (1)
Спасибо (Thak you)	–	\	3 (1)
Хорошо (Well)	–	\	36 (3)
Что (What)	–	V	25 (2)
Я был бы вам очень благодарен (I would be very grateful to you)	–	\	17 (3)

not neutral and non-emotional enough, they could use some acoustic markers, which could also be used in the production of irony. Consequently, the differences between ironic and non-ironic utterances in duration, for example, might be insignificant.

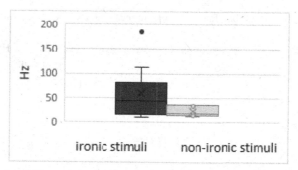

Fig. 2. Boxplot of melodic range in the stressed syllable in well-recognized ironic and non-ironic fragments (by more than 80% of participants).

5 Co-speech Gestures

To better understand the visual cues of irony perception the analysis of co-speech gestures was accomplished. In no case did we pretend to have a comprehensive description of gestures in this material. Our goal was to examine the main types of gestures co-occurring with the nucleus or with the prosodic prominence in both types of sentences. The main interest consisted in establishing the presence or absence of the synchronization between the nucleus and the gesture apex or effort (for the classification and categorization of gestures, see the overview by P. Wagner [1]).

The phenomenon of synchronization has been widely studied, although the results often differ. For some time there was a hypothesis of the so-called "starting point", from which both gestures and speech are planned simultaneously [15]. Nevertheless the recent theories [16, 17] suggest another explanation, assuming that there might be more freedom in the speech and gestures production planning. The difference in synchronization (the precise coincidence with the beginning of the stressed syllable or the late realization of gestures) may be caused by difference in speech planning. Thus, in spontaneous speech the gestures will not co-occur as precisely, as in prepared speech [18]. It lets us expect the high level of synchronization between pitch pattern and gestures in actors' speech. We also analyzed the pitch movement direction in the nucleus and gestures direction.

The analysis showed that all well-recognized ironic and non-ironic utterances (in the experiment with mute video) were synchronized with one of the gestures (Table 3). The direction of the gesture in 100% of cases matched the pitch movement direction in both ironic and non-ironic utterances. The gesture apex co-occurred with the beginning of the nucleus.

78% of the well-recognized ironic utterances were accompanied by head movement, in 36% of phrases a rounding of unrounded vowels was observed, hands and arms movements co-occurred with the nucleus of 21% of utterances with irony, with the same frequency the hyperarticulation was present, as well as the gaze movement. In 86% of ironic utterances various gestures co-occurred.

100% of non-ironic utterances were matched by head movement, one of the phrases was pronounced with eyebrow lifting and one with the gaze movement in the same direction than the pitch movement. The distinctions between ironic and non-ironic gestures

Table 3. Synchronization of gestures and mimics with the nucleus in ironic phrases.

Text of the fragment	Head	Hands/arms	Gaze/eyes	Eyebrows	Lips rounding	Hyperarticulation
Ха-ха (*Ha-ha*)	/		blinking		+	
Гениально (*Genius*)	\					
Сейчас (*Now*)	\		blinking			+
Счастливая семейная жизнь (*Happy family life*)	\	\			+	
Ну это мне совершенно необходимо (*This is absolutely necessary for me*)	\	\	\			
Благородно (*That's precious*)	\					+
Настоящая семейная жизнь (*<It's> the real married life*)	\	\	opening			
Это сенсация (*It's a sensation*)	shaking					
Похвально (*<it's commendable*)	\		blinking			
Ну спасибо (*Oh, thanks*)		opening mov.				+
Спасибо тебе нечеловеческое (*Thank you so much*)	\					
Серьезное дело у нас тут (*This is actually a serious matter*)	\					

(continued)

might be subtle and seem to be more qualitative than quantitative. Though we observed

Table 3. (*continued*)

Text of the fragment	Head	Hands/arms	Gaze/eyes	Eyebrows	Lips rounding	Hyperarticulation
Лечиться значит (*Well, <he's> been treated*)	\				+	
Очень смешно (*Very funny*)	\					
Бедненький (*Poor*)	\			/		+
Молодец (*Well done*)	/		/			+
Да (*Yes*)	V	\	\		+	+
Вот это сырники (*Are these cheese pancakes?*)	/	\	/			
Да неужели (*Really*)			\		+	
Делать мне нечего (*I've nothing to do*)	/				+	

that there was no lip rounding and no hyperarticulation in the non-ironic utterances compared to the ironic phrases.

6 Results and Discussion

The findings of the first two perceptual experiments indicated that informants can successfully identify an irony based on the visual or acoustic cues alone, with no additional lexical or semantic information, 87.5% of the ironic phrases being satisfactorily detected by more than 60% of the participants (see Table 4), mean percentage of correct categorization being 77.8%, standard deviation being 16.8.

Based on the results for the two experiments containing only audial and only visual stimuli, identification of non-ironic utterances by Russian speakers seems to be less successful than that of ironic phrases, the mean percentage of correct recognition for non-ironic stimuli being 64.8% and standard deviation being 22. Only 66.6% of these utterances were satisfactorily classified by more than 60% of the informants.

The difference in the recognition of ironic and non-ironic stimuli in the first perceptual experiment has been found to be statistically significant ($p < 0,05$). In other words, when presented only with video without sound, the participants identified ironic stimuli better than non-ironic ones.

Table 4. The percentage of recognition of ironic phrases in three experiments.

Text of the fragment	Video only (%)	Audio only (%)	Video + Audio (%)
Ха-ха (*Ha-ha*)	77	84	89
Гениально (*Genius*)	97	96	100
Сейчас (*Now*)	94	56	100
Счастливая семейная жизнь (*Happy family life*)	81	96	98
Ну это мне совершенно необходимо (*This is absolutely necessary for me*)	65	52	54
Благородно (*That's precious*)	71	40	80
Настоящая семейная жизнь (*<It's> the real married life*)	65	80	67
Это сенсация (*It's a sensation*)	90	60	91
Похвально (*<it's commendable*)	81	92	65
Ну спасибо (*Oh, thanks*)	68	92	89
Спасибо тебе нечеловеческое (*Thank you so much*)	87	92	85
Серьезное дело у нас тут (*This is actually a serious matter*)	45	56	74
Лечиться значит (*Well, <he's> been treated*)	90	96	98
Очень смешно (*Very funny*)	97	84	98
Бедненький (*Poor*)	97	64	100
Молодец (*Well done*)	81	68	91
Да (*Yes*)	45	60	63
Вот это сырники (*Are these cheese pancakes?*)	97	88	83
Да неужели (*Really*)	94	60	100
Делать мне нечего (*I've nothing to do*)	87	88	94

Both ironic and non-ironic fragments were generally better recognized when the informants were presented with both sound and video. The mean percentage of correct recognition was higher in the third experiment (80% for video with sound (SD: 22) and 72% (SD: 19) and 73% (SD: 22) when presenting only sound and only video, respectively).The differences in the results for the experiment containing audiovisual stimuli and the experiments containing only video and only sound are statistically significant

($p < 0.05$), while there is no statistical difference between recognition of the audial and visual stimuli alone.

The same tendency was observed when comparing the number of well-identified stimuli (correctly categorized by more than 80% of participants); when the informants were presented with the audio and video recordings at the same time, 23 stimuli out of 35 were reliably identified, and when given only sound and only video, 18 and 17 stimuli were reliably recognized, respectively.

An interesting tendency was observed regarding the correlation between the experimental results. The Pearson coefficient of the results of the experiment with visual and audiovisual stimuli was significantly higher than that of the experiment with audial and audiovisual stimuli. On the Chaddock scale, the relationship between the results of the experiment with muted video and the experiment with corresponding simultaneous video and sound is strong (Pearson coefficient = 0.79), while the relationship between the results of the experiment containing audio recordings and the experiment with both video and sound is moderate (Pearson coefficient = 0.49). It applies to both ironic and non-ironic stimuli. These findings might suggest that informants mainly focus on visual rather than acoustic cues of irony.

7 Conclusions

The results of the perception experiments indicate that irony can be recognized successfully despite the absence of context and lexical irony markers. It appears that audial and visual cues of irony are sufficient for the majority of the participants to correctly identify 87.5% of ironic stimuli.

One such cue was found to be the pitch range; the accented syllables of ironic stimuli are characterized by a wider pitch range than those of non-ironic stimuli. While there was no statistical difference in the perception of audio and video recordings, the combination of the two ensured the best result. A strong correlation was found between the results of the first and the third perception experiments, which might indicate that participants primarily focus on visual rather than audial cues of irony while assessing ironic speech.

Up until this point, there have been scant studies devoted to the relationship between acoustic and visual characteristics of ironic speech. Tendencies identified at this early stage of the current study will be further examined using the materials from the extended video and audio corpora of ironic speech.

Despite the close-sourced dataset, the data obtained provide interesting information on irony perception through different channels and on their interaction. It also contributes some new information about variety of actors strategies when expressing irony and about its input on audience perception. These aspects may be of interest for the film industry and can be developed in further research. Acoustic cues of irony could be used in speech synthesis and speech recognition in machine-human dialogue systems. The findings on the interaction of visual and acoustic channels can be considered in AI systems, using the audiovisual interface. Besides, the results of the study can be applied in the fields of forensic phonetics and in second language acquisition.

Acknowledgments. The project "Acoustic correlates of irony with respect to basic types of pitch movement" was supported by the RFBR grant № 20-012-00552.

References

1. Wagner, P., Malisz, S., Kopp, S.: Gesture and speech in interaction: an overview. Speech Commun. **57**, 209–232 (2014)
2. Becker, R., et al.: Aktionsarten, speech and gesture. In: Proceedings of GESPIN2011: Gesture and Speech in Interaction, Bielefeld, Germany (2011)
3. Bergman, K., Aksu, V., Kopp, S.: The relation of speech and gestures: temporal synchrony follows semantic synchrony. In: Proceedings of GESPIN2011: Gesture and Speech in Interaction, Bielefeld, Germany (2011)
4. Aylett, R., Krenn, B., Pelachaud, C., Shimodaira, H. (eds.): IVA 2013. LNCS (LNAI), vol. 8108. Springer, Heidelberg (2013). https://doi.org/10.1007/978-3-642-40415-3
5. Brugman, H., Wittenburg, P., Levinson, S.C., Kita, S.: Multimodal annotations in gesture and sign language studies, In: Third International Conference on Language Resources and Evaluation, pp. 176–182 (2002)
6. Kipp, M.: Multimodal annotation, querying and analysis in ANVIL. In: Multimedia information extraction, pp. 531–368. John Wiley and Sons Inc., Hoboken, NJ (2009)
7. De Ruiter, J.P., Bangerter, A., Dings, P.: Interplay between gesture and speech in the production of referring expressions: investigating the tradeoff hypothesis. Top. Cogn. Sci. **4**(2), 232–248 (2012)
8. Barbulescu, A., Ronfar, R., Bailly, G.: Generative audio-visual prosodic model for virtual actors. In: EEE Engineering in Medicine and Biology Magazine: The Quarterly Magazine of the Engineering in Medicine & Biology Society, pp. 40–51 (2017)
9. Haverkate, H.: A speech act analysis of irony. J. Pragmat. **14**, 77–109 (1990)
10. Skrelin, P., Kochetkova, U., Evdokimova, V., Novoselova, D.: Can we detect irony in speech using phonetic characteristics only? – looking for a methodology of analysis. In: Karpov, A., Potapova, R. (eds.) SPECOM 2020. LNCS (LNAI), vol. 12335, pp. 544–553. Springer, Cham (2020). https://doi.org/10.1007/978-3-030-60276-5_52
11. Kochetkova, U., Skrelin, P., Evdokimova, V., Novoselova, D.: Perception of irony in speech. In: Sherbakova, O. (ed.) Proceedings of the 4th International Conference on Neurobiology of Speech and Language, pp. 72–73. Skifia-Print, Saint Petersburg (2020)
12. Cutler, A.: On saying what you mean without meaning what you say. In: Proceedings from the 10th Regional Meeting of the Chicago Linguistic Society, pp. 117–123. CLS, Chicago (1974)
13. Niebuhr, O.: Rich reduction: Sound-segment residuals and the encoding of communicative functions along the hypo-hyper scale. In: 7th Tutorial and Research Workshop on Experimental Linguistics, pp. 11–24. St. Petersburg, Russia (2016)
14. Cheang, H., Pell, M.: Acoustic markers of sarcasm in Cantonese and English. J. Acoust. Soc. Am. **126**(3), 1394–1405 (2009)
15. McNeill, D.: Hand and Mind: What Gestures Reveal about Thought. University of Chicago Press, Chicago (1992)
16. Loehr, D.: Temporal, structural, and pragmatic synchrony between intonation and gesture. In: Laboratory Phonology. Journal of the Association for Laboratory Phonology **3**, 71–89 (2012)
17. Chui, K.: Temporal patterning of speech and iconic gestures in conversational discourse. J. Pragmat. **37**, 871–887 (2005)
18. Grishina, E.A.: Russkaia Gestikulatsia s Lingvisticheskoi Tochki Zrenia [Russian Gesticulation from the Liguistic Point of View]. Iazyki Slavianskoi Kulturi, Moscow (2017). (in Russian)

Findings of Biomedical Russian to English Machine Translation Competition

Elizaveta Ezhergina[1] , Mariia Fedorova[1(✉)] , Valentin Malykh[2],
and Daria Petrova[3]

[1] MiraMedix, Moscow, Russia
maria.fjodorowa@gmail.com
[2] Kazan Federal University, Kazan, Russia
[3] Higher School of Economics, Moscow, Russia
petrova.s.daria@gmail.com

Abstract. Translation of medical texts is a complex task that requires usage of models specifically trained for the biomedical domain. In this paper we present the dataset, metrics, and baselines used for the Biomedical Russian-English Machine Translation competition. We describe dataset collection and markup along with baseline development and participants' models. The collected dataset is available by the link https://github.com/MariaFjodorowa/MedMTEval/tree/main/data.

1 Introduction

The overwhelming ocean of textual information is created nowadays annually. Most of the information is created in the English language, thus making the task of machine translation of primary importance.

The task of machine translation in the biomedical domain presents a particular challenge, as biomedical texts typically contain features that are unique to this field (i.e. abundance of abbreviations, inconsistency in usage of terms) which makes the regular machine translation engines insufficient.

In order to solve this issue, it is necessary to use models trained and fine-tuned specifically on biomedical data which presents another challenge: collection and processing of such data in a way that does not violate privacy of patients' medical information and at the same time provides consistency in the translation and the markup of domain-related words and expressions in different languages. Moreover, it is also preferable to have data that are rich both in scientific domain-related terms and in basic vocabulary, as the imbalance of these subtypes might result in model's incapability to translate text coherently.

The goal of our contest is to research and develop possible solutions for the task of medical machine translation between Russian and English language. In this paper we explore the preparation steps, the process, and the results of this contest. In Sect. 2 we provide description of the dataset and its markup process; in Sect. 3 we describe our baseline models along with participants' systems and their training and evaluation; the last two sections are focused on the results of the competition, conclusions, and the possible subsequent work.

© The Author(s), under exclusive license to Springer Nature Switzerland AG 2022
V. Malykh and A. Filchenkov (Eds.): AINL 2022, CCIS 1731, pp. 95–101, 2022.
https://doi.org/10.1007/978-3-031-23372-2_9

2   Dataset

The dataset provided for the participants consists of pairs of sentences and paragraphs from medical texts in Russian and English. The training slice contains 2995 such pairs and the testing part contains 353 pairs. Sources of the data for training include the official website of WHO, abstracts of scientific biomedical papers, and patient descriptions (digital health records).

The diversity of data is of key importance because it has been found out that upon the usage of completely scientifically-worded texts (i.e. only biomedical papers) the models demonstrated good results in translation of medical terms, but performed rather poorly on more coherent but less scientifically-oriented texts (i.e. anamneses or articles for regular readers who do not have medical education). For the test dataset, all English texts were taken from synthetic patient descriptions from TREC 2021 Clinical Trials contest[1] [15].

2.1   Markup Process

The patient descriptions were annotated in two ways: at first they were translated into Russian via DeepL engine[2]. The resulted translations were verified by an assessor. Then a named entities markup was performed for medical terms in order to count how many of them have been translated correctly. We used Label Studio environment[3] [17] for both types of annotation. The processed dataset is available by the link https://github.com/MariaFjodorowa/MedMTEval/tree/main/data.

The main challenges of the translations' verification were different naming conventions across languages and the fact that doctors use contractions and abbreviations in electronic health records instead of full words and expressions typically present in the medical literature. This often results in difference in length and overall text complexity between the Russian translation and the English one. One of the possible reasons for this may be the fact that in the English language, constructions with a noun as an attribute are more easily distributed due to their simpler structure. Another reason for this might be the fact that English typically uses more abbreviations compared to Russian. And thus, there may be no abbreviation equivalent to English in Russian. As for other differences in the two languages, considering the adjectives it may be unclear what an attribute refers to because, unlike in Russian, adjectives in English do not change either by gender, or by number, or by case.

In addition, some difficulties arise if the medical abbreviation has several decodings: the context may not be enough to determine which meaning is implied (for example, when listing illnesses in the patient's past history: MI may refer to myocardial infarction or mitral insufficiency).

Another point of complexity is that one disease can have several names, and if they are equally often used in speech then the choice of translation remains mainly for the annotator. Examples are: history - анамнез/история болезни, HTN

---

[1] https://trec.nist.gov/data/trials2021.html.

[2] https://deepl.com/translator.

[3] https://labelstud.io/.

> English: Cerebral angiography further revealed patent right ACA and MCA and patent left ACA and left MCA.
>
> Russian: Церебральная ангиография также выявила патентные правую переднюю и среднюю мозговые артерии и патентные левые переднюю и среднюю мозговые артерии.

Fig. 1. Example of a longer Russian translation.

– гипертония/(артериальная) гипертензия/АГ, HPV – папилломавирусы человека (ПВЧ)/вирусы папилломы человека (ВПЧ). An example translation result is presented in Fig. 1.

The named entities markup has been done as follows: a fine-tuned BioBERT [10] model extracted treatments, conditions and some measurements from the texts and a human assessor with a medical education fixed the errors. The CHIA [9] biomedical corpus was used for training the model. An example of the named entities markup is shown in Fig. 2.

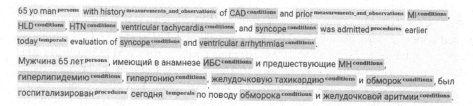

Fig. 2. Example of the named entities markup on the same text in two languages: English (top) and Russian (bottom).

3   Solutions

3.1   Baselines

The baseline of the project was presented by three machine translation engines. The first one is DeepL which is openly available on the corresponding website. There is no information neither on its exact architecture nor on the data used for its training, but it is most likely a transformer model trained on vast amounts of data. The second is a transformer model by Helsinki-NLP [16]. It is based on MarianMT system [8] and is available as part of Transformers library by HuggingFace [18]. It is applied directly, i.e. without any fine-tuning. The third baseline is the same Helsinki-NLP model additionally trained on the corpora from Biomedical translation tasks of WMT 2020 [3] and WMT 2021 [19] (fine-tuned MarianMT). These datasets contain the abstracts from scientific papers only (6920 pairs from both WMT competitions in total). The model was trained for 10 epochs with default parameters.

3.2   Participant Solutions

The first participant (shershulya) translated the training dataset with a "teacher model", counted the Translation Edit Rate of the results, and excluded the training samples with a high TER score (e.g. the WHO data could contain mistakes since they were collected automatically. The teacher model was an ensemble of 6 LSTM models trained from scratch and averaged their predictions during decoding. The input was BPE tokens with Cyrillic words transliterated into the Latin one. Each LSTM model was initialized randomly. After removing the problem samples from the dataset, the same architecture was trained as a "student model".

The second participant (c00k1ez) trained the baseline MarianMT model for 40 epochs on the data provided and some additional data. He parsed names of drugs and diseases from a drug reference guide[4] and English-Russian wordlists[56]. Surprisingly, this has not improved the metrics. Future experiments can include two-stage fine-tuning (tuning the baseline on full-text training data first, then tuning it on the names of drugs and diseases) and putting the names of drugs and diseases into some contexts.

4   Metrics

The primary metric used for the evaluation of results was COMET [14]. It was calculated with the assistance of wmt21-cometinho-da model presented in [14] which is a regression model trained on Direct Assessments corpora from WMT15 to WMT20 [1, 2,4–7] using a lightweight encoder model. The choice of COMET as the main metric was made because it can handle synonyms and has no lower and upper bounds and thus is suitable for ranking translations and comparing models, having high correlations with human judgments.

Other metrics used in evaluating models' performance include BLEU [13], ROUGE-L-F1 [11]. These two metrics are based on n-gram comparison of a translation and multiple possible references. Last but not the least, we used a metric for entity recognition accuracy (NER-acc). It is calculated with regard to medicine-related entities like medical conditions and measurements, drugs, etc. NER-acc is a lemma-based exact match, meaning it denotes the number of the entities that have been translated properly, having been given the lemmatized named entities. To calculate the metric, we used only lemmas with the specific part-of-speech tags, namely proper noun, verb, noun, and adjective. For morphological analysis, scispacy package [12] was used, since some words, e.g. prepositions, can vary in hypotheses and references without changing the meaning of a term.

5   Competition Results

Over the course of almost two months, 27 participants joined the competition. Unfortunately, only two of the participants allowed us to publish their results on the final

---

[4] https://www.vidal.ru/.

[5] https://www.homeenglish.ru/otherbol.htm.

[6] https://s-english.ru/leksika/illnesses-and-diseases.

leaderboard (presented at Table 1). Their submissions surpassed two of the baselines: both beat the plain MarianMT model and one managed to reach results higher than the fine-tuned MarianMT model.

The usage of DeepL engine for the creation of the dataset leads to an unfair advantage for it in the final scores. Even if it uses two separate models for different translation directions and not a multilingual one, these models were possibly trained on the same dataset and thus tend to choose particular words if there exists a range of correct translations for some terms (e.g. Erythrocytes and Red blood cells).

Table 1. Biomedical Russian to english machine translation competition results.

#	Method\Metric	COMET	BLEU	NER-acc	ROUGE-L-F1
1	DeepL	0.7834	0.4470	0.8078	0.7129
2	shershulya (Daniil Lukichev)	0.7452	0.4175	0.7976	0.6950
3	fine-tuned MarianMT	0.6752	0.4030	0.7358	0.6805
4	c00k1ez (Egor Plotnikov)	0.6581	0.3912	0.6979	0.6703
5	MarianMT	0.5010	0.2780	0.6286	0.5770

But, even with this advantage, DeepL does not beat the best result from WMT21 biomedical track, which is 0.4918 BLEU [19]. We suppose that translating electronic health records is a more difficult task than translating abstracts of (biomedical) scientific papers.

The vanilla MarianMT had, unsurprisingly, the worst performance because of the lack of medical terms in its training data. Examples of its mistakes and comparison with the tuned model's output can be found in Table 2. The common problems are incorrect translations of abbreviations (row 1), usage of transliterations and repetitions instead of unknown words (row 2), entirely wrong terms (row 3), mistakes with homonyms (row 4), repetitions in cases of two words with similar meaning one after another (row 5), grammar mistakes (row 6) and even wrong translations of some non-medical words (row 7). As can be seen, fine-tuning the transformer on medical texts solves some of these problems.

Both baseline models handle typos successfully: "мазьлокального примее-нения" ("ointmenttopical usaage") is almost correctly translated as "ointment", while the correct answer is "topical ointment") which should be because of their sentence-piece encoding. However, this encoding is also a source of problems, e.g. "живот" ("abdomen") is translated as "animal" ("животное") by both models.

Interestingly, the orderings for all the used metrics are the same, which means that for our task COMET is highly correlated with BLEU and ROUGE. Surprisingly, all the other metrics are correlated with NER-acc, we can conclude that accuracy in entity naming translation depends on the translation of the whole text and it is not required to have specific handling for this specific task.

Table 2. Baselines' translation mistakes.

#	Source	Target	MarianMT	Fine-tuned MarianMT
1	МНО	INR	MONEY	MON
2	антитела	antibodies	anti-anttels	antibodies
3	очаговая болезненность	focal tenderness	occipital pain	focal tenderness
4	стеснение в груди	chest tightening	a shy chest	chest tightness
5	нежный и мягкий	tender and soft	soft and soft	soft and soft
6	Ее вес	Her weight	Its weight	Her weight
7	упитанный	well-nourished	well-taught	well-nourished

6   Conclusion

The competition demonstrated that transfer learning of non-specific domain-oriented models with the usage of varied biomedical data can be a successful approach, even though the influence of topical data skew can be observed in some of the translations made by the resulting models. One of the main issues stemming from this is the model's incapability to predict a correct translation for a relatively simple word that does not belong to the biomedical field that sometimes appears in the results. In order to eliminate such flaws an enhancement might be done to the suggested training dataset: perhaps providing a share of texts that are less scientifically inclined and using more basic vocabulary should be helpful in correction of this skew.

The competition is going on and it is still possible to enroll at the website: https://codalab.lisn.upsaclay.fr/competitions/1856. There is no planned end date for it (as to the date of the publication). The evaluation script useful for the participation can be found at https://github.com/MariaFjodorowa/MedMTEval.

Acknowledgments. The authors are thankful to Aleksandr Kokovikhin who has done the markup for medical named entities manually.

References

1. Barrault, L., et al.: Findings of the 2020 conference on machine translation (WMT20). In: Proceedings of the Fifth Conference on Machine Translation, pp. 1–55. Association for Computational Linguistics (2020)
2. Barrault, L., et al.: Findings of the 2019 conference on machine translation (wmt19). In: Proceedings of the Fourth Conference on Machine Translation (Volume 2: Shared Task Papers, Day 1), pp. 1–61 (2019)
3. Bawden, R., et al.: Findings of the WMT 2020 biomedical translation shared task: Basque, Italian and Russian as new additional languages. In: Proceedings of the Fifth Conference on Machine Translation, pp. 660–687. Association for Computational Linguistics (2020)
4. Bojar, O., et al.: Findings of the 2016 conference on machine translation. In: Proceedings of the First Conference on Machine Translation: Volume 2, Shared Task Papers, pp. 131–198, Berlin, Germany. Association for Computational Linguistics (2016)

5. Bojar, O., et al.: Findings of the 2015 workshop on statistical machine translation. In: Proceedings of the Tenth Workshop on Statistical Machine Translation, Lisbon, Portugal, pp. 1–46. Association for Computational Linguistics (2015)
6. Bojar, O., et al.: Findings of the 2018 conference on machine translation (WMT18). In: Proceedings of the Third Conference on Machine Translation: Shared Task Papers, Belgium, Brussels, pp. 272–303. Association for Computational Linguistics (2018)
7. Bojar, O., et al.: Findings of the 2017 conference on machine translation (wmt17). In: Proceedings of the Second Conference on Machine Translation, Volume 2: Shared Task Papers, Copenhagen, Denmark, pp. 169–214. Association for Computational Linguistics (2017)
8. Junczys-Dowmunt, M., et al.: Marian: fast neural machine translation in C++. In: Proceedings of ACL 2018, System Demonstrations, Melbourne, Australia, pp. 116–121. Association for Computational Linguistics (2018)
9. Kury, F., et al.: Chia, a large annotated corpus of clinical trial eligibility criteria. Sci. Data 7(1), 1–11 (2020)
10. Lee, J., et al.: BioBERT: a pre-trained biomedical language representation model for biomedical text mining. Bioinformatics 36(4), 1234–1240 (2020)
11. Lin, C. Y.: Rouge: a package for automatic evaluation of summaries. In: Proceedings of the ACL Workshop: Text Summarization Braches Out 2004, p. 10 (2004)
12. Neumann, M., King, D., Beltagy, I., Ammar, W.: ScispaCy: fast and robust models for biomedical natural language processing. In: Proceedings of the 18th BioNLP Workshop and Shared Task, Florence, Italy, pp. 319–327. Association for Computational Linguistics (2019)
13. Papineni, K., Roukos, S., Ward, T., Zhu, W.J.: Bleu: a method for automatic evaluation of machine translation. In: Proceedings of the 40th Annual Meeting of the Association for Computational Linguistics, pp. 311–318 (2002)
14. Rei, R., Stewart, C., Farinha, A.C., Lavie, A.: COMET: a neural framework for MT evaluation. In: Proceedings of the 2020 Conference on Empirical Methods in Natural Language Processing (EMNLP), pp. 2685–2702. Association for Computational Linguistics (2020)
15. Soboroff, I.: Overview of TREC 2021. In: 30th Text REtrieval Conference. Gaithersburg, Maryland (2021)
16. Tiedemann, J., Thottingal, S.: OPUS-MT - building open translation services for the world. In: Proceedings of the 22nd Annual Conference of the European Association for Machine Translation, Lisboa, Portugal, pp. 479–480. European Association for Machine Translation (2020)
17. Tkachenko, M., Malyuk, M., Shevchenko, N., Holmanyuk, A., Liubimov, N.: Label Studio: Data labeling software (2020–2022). Open source software https://github.com/heartexlabs/label-studio
18. Wolf, T., et al.: Transformers: state-of-the-art natural language processing. In: Proceedings of the 2020 Conference on Empirical Methods in Natural Language Processing: System Demonstrations, pp. 38–45. Association for Computational Linguistics (2020)
19. Yeganova, L., et al.: Findings of the WMT 2021 biomedical translation shared task: summaries of animal experiments as new test set. In: Proceedings of the Sixth Conference on Machine Translation, pp. 664–683. Association for Computational Linguistics (2021)

Translation of Medical Texts with Ensembling and Knowledge Distillation

Daniil Lukichev[✉]

Higher School of Economics, Moscow, Russia
`dalukichev@edu.hse.ru`

Abstract. Knowledge distillation describes a way to train a student network to perform better by learning from a more powerful teacher network. We show that the performance of a teacher consisting of an ensemble of 6 models can be achieved with the help of a student consisting of one model, which leads to significantly faster decoding and a large increase in the quality of the model. In our approach to distilling knowledge, we translate the full training dataset using the teacher model to use the translations as additional knowledge for the student network. For the translation of biomedical texts containing a large number of specific nested named entities, the byte-pair encoding approach was chosen, which also improved the quality of the model.

1 Introduction

Knowledge distillation describes the idea of improving student networks by matching their predictions with those of a stronger teacher network. There are two ways to use knowledge distillation for neural machine translation (NMT): First, the student network can be a model with fewer layers and hidden units. The main purpose is to reduce the model size of NMT systems without significant loss of translation quality. Second, without changing the model architecture, reasonable gains can be obtained by combining different models of the same architecture with an ensemble.

We show that the performance of a teacher consisting of 6 models can be achieved by a student consisting of a single model, resulting in significantly faster decoding and smaller memory footprint. In our knowledge distillation method, we translate the full training data using the teacher model to use the translation as additional training data for the student network.

A separate problem of the dataset presented at the competition for the translation of medical texts was the presence of nested named entities, many of which occurred only once or twice in the dataset. Despite the fact that it is possible to single out a complete list of named entities found in the dataset, the specificity of biomedical terminology is that there is an amazing number of variations for any given object. For example, PSA, C4 PTS, C4 PEPCase refer to the same object. In addition, some objects, such as proteins and genes, can naturally take up less

V. Malykh and A. Filchenkov (Eds.): AINL 2022, CCIS 1731, pp. 102–107, 2022.
https://doi.org/10.1007/978-3-031-23372-2_10

"words" (for example, HA and APG12 are separate proteins in pHA-APG12). To preserve such nested named entities, an approach based not on words, but on subwords was chosen. Therefore, byte-pair encoding was chosen for encoding the dictionary.

2   Related Work

(Ba and Caruana, 2014) showed that feedforward shallow networks can learn complex functions previously studied by deep networks by extracting knowledge. In the TIMIT phoneme recognition and CIFAR-10 image recognition tasks, small networks similar to deeper convolutional models can be trained.

(Hinton et al., 2015) proposed knowledge distillation for image classification (MNIST) and acoustic modeling. They show that nearly all improvements achieved by training an ensemble of deep neural networks can be distilled in a single neural network of the same size

(Sennrich et al., 2016) describes the use of byte-pair encoding for neural machine learning. Russian must be translated into the Latin alphabet in order to use the byte-encoding of the Russian language effectively.

(Freitag et al., 2017) demonstrates an ensemble distillation approach. They also show that the quality of the model improves if you augment the text data with additional text that was translated by the model itself.

(Sheng and Natarajan, 2018) describes an approach for byte encoding of subwords for biomedical texts. They show that this approach allows you to preserve unique named entities that appear specifically in medical texts.

3   Data Preparation

The data provided at the competition for the translation of medical texts is used as a dataset. The number of pairs of sentences in the training sample is 2300. To improve the quality of the model, data from previous years' medical text translation competitions (WMT-2020, WMT-2021) were added to the training sample. The final volume of the training sample was 9,500 pairs of Russian-English sentences.

For Russian translation, we cannot effectively use common vocabulary to learn BPE because the alphabet is different. Therefore, we follow the approach described in (Sennrich et al., 2016) by first mapping Russian text to Latin characters via ISO-9 transliteration, then learning the BPE operation on the concatenation of English and Latinized Russian training data, and then applying the BPE operation Maps back to Cyrillic. We apply Latin BPE operations to English data (training data and input), and Cyrillic and Latin BPE operations to Russian data.

Several sentences were found in the dataset that had several correct translations, which differed in the choice and order of words. Network training becomes more complicated if the training corpus contains noisy pairs of sentences or sentences with several correct translations. In our work, we translate complete parallel data using our teacher model. This gives us the opportunity to evaluate each translation using a link to the original. We are removing offers with high TER scores (Snover et al., 2006) from our training data. By removing noisy or inaccessible pairs of sentences, the training algorithm is able to train a stronger network. For example, pair «ru» :«Однако для ликвидаци ивсех форм насилия в отношении детей необходимо, чтобы страте гии INSPIRE были лучше интегрированы в существующие национальн ые системыи пользовались более широкой поддержкой со стороны государства.», «en»: «However, INSPIRE strategies should be better integrated into existing national frameworks and more widely supported by governments in order to end all forms of violence against children.» had high TER score and was removed from training dataset.

4   Description of the Approach

4.1   Byte-Pair Encoding

We segment words using byte pair encoding (BPE) (Sennrich et al., 2016). BPE, originally developed as a compression algorithm (Gage, 1994), is suitable for word segmentation as follows: First, each word in the training dictionary is represented as a sequence of characters plus the end of the word symbol. All characters are added to the character dictionary. Then determine the most common pair of characters and combine all its occurrences to add a new character to the dictionary. Repeat the previous step until the specified number of merge operations have been checked. BPE starts with character-level segmentation, but as the number of merge operations increases, it becomes increasingly different from pure character-level models by encoding common strings or even whole words into a single character. This allows you to trade off the size of the model dictionary and the length of the training sequence. The ordered list of merge operations learned on the training set can be applied to any text to split words into dictionary-like units of subwords relative to the training set. To improve the consistency of source and target text segmentation, we combine the source and target parts of the training set to learn BPE.

4.2   Single Model Description

Our student systems are attentional encoder-decoder networks (Bahdanau et al., 2015). We use minibatches of size 80, a maximum sentence length of 50, word embeddings of size 500, and hidden layers of size 1024. Gradient norm is clipped to 1.0. Models are trained with Adadelta (Zeiler, 2012), reshuffling the training corpus between epochs. Due to resource limitations, we did not train ensemble components independently, which could result in more diverse models and better ensembles. Decoding is performed with beam search with a beam size of 12.

4.3   Knowledge Distillation

The idea of knowledge distillation is to match the predictions of a student network to that of a teacher network. In this work, we collect the predictions of the teacher network by translating the full training data with the teacher network. By doing this, we produce a new reference for the training data which can be used by the student network to simulate the teacher network. There are two ways of using the forward translation. First, we can train the student network only on the original source and the translations. Secondly, we can add the translations as additional training data to the original training data. This has the side effect that the final training data size of the student network is doubled. Since the translation of this additional data was made in the backward direction, it gave a good result and increased the final score.

4.4   Ensemble Teacher Model

An ensemble of different NMT models can improve the translation performance of NMT systems. The idea is to train multiple models in parallel and combine their predictions by averaging each model's probability at each time step during decoding. In this work, we use an ensemble of 6 models as the teacher model. All 6 separate systems are trained on the same parallel data and use the same optimization method. The only difference is the random initialization of the parameters.

5   Evaluation and Results

5.1   Single Teacher Model

Instead of using a stronger teacher model, we use the same model for both the student network and the teacher network. Using direct translation, we can stabilize the student network and make its solution much stronger. The results are shown in Table 1. The right column shows the result obtained on the test dataset. The COMET metric (Rei et al., 2020) was chosen as the metric for the final evaluation of the model quality, because it is provided by the competition. Data distillation adds 0.3 points if train the model with continuation and 0.4 points if train the model from scratch.

5.2   Ensemble Teacher Model

The results of using an ensemble of 6 models as a teacher model are summarized in Table 2. Using only direct translation improves the quality of the model compared to the previous ones by 0.1 point of the COMET metric. Further, the same dependence can be traced as before: the distillation of data adds to the quality, and the model shows itself better if it is trained from scratch. Using only the forward translation improves the single system by 0.2 points in COMET. When using both the original reference and the forward translation, we get an additional improvement of 0.25 points in COMET. The final quality of the model is 0.745 points. This approach gave a good result on the COMET metric and was chosen as the final one.

Table 1. Knowledge distillation based on a single teacher model with same architecture and dimensions as the student networks.

Setup	Data	From scratch	Continue training	COMET score
Single model	Original (9K)	✓		0.66
Distillation	Translation ens (9K)	✓		0.68
			✓	0.67
	Translation baseline + original (18K)	✓		0.70
			✓	0.69

Table 2. Knowledge distillation based on a ensemble teacher model.

Setup	Data	From scratch	Continue training	COMET score
ensemble of 6	Original (9K)	✓		0.72
Distillation	Translation ens (9K)	✓		0.738
			✓	0.732
	Translation ens + original (18K)	✓		0.745
			✓	0.741

6   Conclusion

Since one of the baselines of the competition was a strong pre-trained api for machine translation from deepl, our solution lagged slightly behind it in the comet score (by 0.4 points). But many translations of sentences and complex nested named entities in the test sample coincide with those proposed by our model, given that our model was not pre-trained, but was retrained for the task of machine translation, unlike deepl, this can be considered a success. For example NERs like Hyperlipidemia or Turgor either do not occur in the training sample, or they occur, but in a modified form, but were translated correctly by our model as well as by the deepl api. Some abbreviations were translated more correctly by our model. For example, PT (Prothrombin Time), was translated by deepl api as PTV (since the abbreviation in Russian consists of three letters «ПТВ»), our model translated this abbreviation correctly as PT.

In this paper, we show our different approaches to solving the competition for the translation of medical texts.We show that data distillation improves the quality of the machine translation model in any case, even for an ordinary teacher-student model. We apply the distillation of knowledge to teacher-student model consisting of ensemble of 6 neural networks. In this case, the distillation of knowledge gives a good increase to the points of the COMET metric. In addition to distilling knowledge, we use byte-pair encoding to solve the problem of specific medical named entities, and at the data preprocessing stage, we get rid of sentences that have a low TER-score. The final solution was chosen the teacher-student model with ensemble of 6 models.

References

Ba, J., Caruana, R.: Do deep nets really need to be deep? In: NIPS (2014)

Bahdanau, D., Cho, K., Bengio, Y.: Neural machine translation by jointly learning to align and translate. CoRR, abs/1409.0473 (2015)

Freitag, M., Al-Onaizan, Y., Sankaran, B.: Ensemble distillation for neural machine translation. ArXiv, abs/1702.01802 (2017)

Gage, P.: A new algorithm for data compression. C Users J. Arch. **12**, 23–38 (1994)

Hinton, G., Vinyals, O., Dean, J.: Distilling the knowledge in a neural network. ArXiv, abs/1503.02531 (2015)

Rei, R., Stewart, C., Farinha, A.C., Lavie, A.: COMET: A neural framework for MT evaluation. In: EMNLP (2020)

Sennrich, R., Haddow, B., Birch, A.: Neural machine translation of rare words with subword units. ArXiv, abs/1508.07909 (2016)

Sheng, E., Natarajan, P.: A byte-sized approach to named entity recognition. ArXiv, abs/1809.08386 (2018)

Snover, M., Dorr, B., Schwartz, R., Micciulla, L., Makhoul, J.: A study of translation edit rate with targeted human annotation. In: AMTA (2006)

Zeiler, M. D.: Adadelta: an adaptive learning rate method. ArXiv, abs/1212.5701 (2012)

Author Index

Printed in the United States
by Baker & Taylor Publisher Services

Printed in the United States
by Baker & Taylor Publisher Services